THE PHILOSOPHY OF SHRI BHAGAVAD GITA

THE PHILOSOPHY OF SHRI BHAGAVAD GITA

Ajay Shukla

GYAN PUBLISHING HOUSE
New Delhi-110002

THE PHILOSOPHY OF SHRI BHAGVAD GITA

(Religious Studies)

ISBN : 81-212-0608-1

Published in 2001 in India by
Gyan Publishing House
5, Ansari Road
New Delhi 110 002
Phones : 3282060, 3261060 Fax : 3285914
E-mail : gyanbook@del2.vsnl.net.in
Visit Our Web Site At http:\\www.gyanbooks.com

Laser Typesetting: Grow Computers, Delhi
Printed at: Mehra Offset Press, New Delhi

CONTENTS

INTRODUCTION

I was nineteen when I first read system of Bhagavad Gita, out of my own curiosity. The formal system of education somehow does not teach us anything about the virtues of our own heritage. In the name of secularism the society seems to be almost apologetic of its own roots.

Reading Gita was a mind opener for me. I found the philosophy of Gita of profound practical value and relevance, both at the individual and social levels. I was struck by the power of logic of its philosophy, its scientific outlòok, its analysis of human nature and the spirit of rationality.

Indian philosophy predates the concept of religion itself. The philosophy of Gita is not for any particular sect or religion, it is for human unkind as such. There is no indoctrination in Gita. There is no desire to streamline or bind human behaviour to a code. Instead Gita is set to liberate the individual from all bonds. A way is shown to the individual to free himself from all the mental dilemmas and doubts. In fact several ways are shown for such liberation.

The liberal approach and universality of thought expressed in Gita was moving and it makes Gita socially relevant to modern also. Although the various concepts of Gita have been discussed in detail in this book, I would however like to just briefly mention about one of them which is extremely important for the country as well as the society today. This is the concept of *sambhava* sameness of attitude, to all people and to all situations and it embraces as well as precedes the concepts of social co-existence and secularism as understood in modern times.

Gita accepts that there are different ways to achieve salvation, and different people can achieve the Supreme Being in different ways depending upon their nature. That is to say one can be an idol worshipper and another one may not, and yet both may achieve the same end, simply by doing their duties rightfully. Different people can follow different ways to attain salvation, without one becoming superior to the other. Today we certainly need to spread this message of peaceful co-existence of different faiths.

Gita does not expect uniformity or equality. It is impossible for everyone to be same or equal. Variation is inherent in nature. What is required however is that one should accept these variations as facets and parts of the grand cosmic design which emanates out of a single source, *Brahma*.

The present day issues had already been envisaged and a solution had been provided in Gita. The philosophy of Gita is as relevant today as it was in ancient times, both at the individual and social levels. In fact whereas the center of address in Gita is the individual, it does not advocate individualism. The individual is always viewed in the context of the society and Gita holds that only what is good for the society as a whole can be good for the individual. No wonder Mahatma Gandhi always said that Gita was his source of inspiration.

At the individual level Gita helps one to introspect, to realise one's position in the cosmic design and to get rid of the bonds of attachments and ego complexes. Worries, fears, doubts and dilemmas are the most common afflictions of the individual in modern society. Most of these problems persist because we are unable to view them with a holistic perspective. We are too much involved with ourselves and with what is superficially apparent. We remain ensconced in our parochial vision and hence are unable to see the reality behind the apparent. Gita helps us to clear our vision.

I found that the philosophy of Gita has tremendous practical utility in an ordinary person's social as well as personal life, and in my own way, I have tried to implement the same in my day-to-day working.

Over the years I read and reread Gita, and found new meanings for different situations and new ways to cope with the situations. Gita helped me to introspect, to understand myself and to interpret my actions and my realisation of self. It enriched the quality of my being and has remained my source of strength and inspiration in the moments of despair and darkness.

Indian philosophy has provided infrastructure of thought for all philosophies, religious or otherwise. It would be unfair to relegate Gita as a book of just Hinduism or mythology. It is for mankind as a whole. As such I felt it necessary to make my own effort and contribute to make Gita accessible to all. It was imperative to make things simpler, rational and relevant to our times. This book is an essay in that direction.

In this book it has been my endeavour to achieve the following :

- To trace the development of human thought from origin of the existence to the culmination of Indian philosophy in the form of Gita.
- To explain and discuss the various concepts of the Indian philosophy which preceded Gita, i.e., the Vedas and the Upanishads.
- To discuss the philosophy of Gita in the simplest of the terms.
- To re-examine the concepts of Gita on the anvil of rational and scientific analysis, without accepting any precondition of divinity.

- To find how the concepts of Gita actually work in day to day life, and how they can be of use to an ordinary individual in modern times.
- To discuss apparent contradictions in the philosophy of Gita where they appear.
- To make the reader think and introspect.
- To provide an easy translation of the text of Bhagavad Gita.

The idea is that one who is reading Gita for the first time is also able to read it smoothly and understand the core of its philosophy without the obstructions of the floral trappings. I must accept that in such a surgeon's exercise the poetic beauty of Gita is lost, but then the choice was between the content and the cosmetics and I have chosen the keep the content.

It must also be remembered that there are no exactly equivalent English words for many philosophical terms like *dharma, maya, karma, prakrati jagat,* etc. Depending upon the context, their nearest appropriate equivalents have been used. At places alternative words have also been given to indicate the scope of the meaning.

Every age will interpret Gita according to its own times and situation and will find new meanings, new inspirations and strength to cope up with newer situations. Different people will similarly find different meanings in Gita. That is because the philosophy of Gita is holistic and eternally dynamic. Maybe at times I have also interpreted Gita differently. According to my own thinking and nature, I have tried to be objective, open-minded, scientific and logical. Any other way would not carry my conviction.

Only what is logical can be sacred, not the other way round. Just as I have unaccepted anything only because it is written in some scripture, I would like the readers to be similarly open-minded in their study of Gita.

Ajay Shukla

1

ORIGIN AND DEVELOPMENT OF HUMAN THOUGHT

According to science and Hindu Scriptures in the beginning it was all dark everywhere and matter did not exist. All that existed was energy. When it was so is unknown. What existed, and for how long it remained so is also unknown. Then there was an explosion, an outburst of energy, a discharge of power out of something not yet known or comprehensible. Some of the energy gradually coalesced and matter was formed. The speculation of science is the big bang theory, which describes this phenomenon as the explosion of the black hole.

The Vedas and Upanishads describe this occurrence poetically as the awakening of *Brahma*, as *Brahma* manifesting himself out of his dormancy (sleep). Rig-Veda says that out of his own volition and power, *Brahma* transformed from his non-being state to being state, causing creation of this existence, out of himself. That is why *Brahma* is the creation as well as the cause of creation.

How this matter got formed into millions of balls, got scattered trillions of miles apart, how they started moving in set orbits, how galaxies were formed, and how some of these bodies of matter got lit up and became self luminous stars (suns), all these wonders will remain the quest of science for ever. Even if we ever come to know how it all happened, we will still never know why it did happen so at all. As of now we can only conjecture through science that the entire existence had a common source of origin.

The planet was cooling and its matter was settling down. There were chemicals and chemical reactions. In a few million years things took shape. There were land and water, and there were the celestial bodies all around, the sun, the moon and the stars. And it was all very quiet and lonely. At that time there was no life on the earth. Billions of years back it was so, and remained so for millions of years.

Then, in the backwaters of some ocean somewhere, without any known provocation, a group of amino-nucleic acids suddenly moved forward on their own. They repeated the process and survived in the attempt. Initially they wavered between the living and the non-living forms. Then something made them capable of continuing existence in the living form.

Something also made them perpetuate their existence in the living form as distinct from the non-living form in which they earlier were. And so life came into being, out of a dynamic chemical process. The greatest event of all times, origin of life, had occurred, without causing even a whimper anywhere.

Once come into being as a life form, these clusters of chemicals started changing themselves, started adjusting themselves for survival. That was the beginning of the process of evolution. The primeval life forms evolved continuously, improving and adopting themselves in the process of evolution with a single objective, to be in a better position to survive. Ever since then, the spirit to survive has continuously strengthened and carried the process of evolution ahead.

Origin of Human Thought

The instinct to survive is the most basic character of all living beings. It has been the single most important factor in the process of evolution and the most important cause of the development of body and mind in all life forms. It is only because of this deeply ingrained character (instinct) in every single living cell today that we have all the plant and animal life on this planet. All this phenomenon of life that we see on earth today is nothing but a manifestation of the endeavour of that instinct to survive.

The quest for survival was the guiding principle in the process of evolution of the body and mind. Life forms took up strange and fierce shapes. In order to survive they had to be fit, for fight or for flight. Life was nasty brutish and short. Things were quite insecure. Single cellular beings evolved into complex multi-cellular beings. Division of work within the body developed with different organs doing different works to make the body more fit to survive. Life forms gradually developed sensory organs. Development of sense of perception led to development of memory. Then developed sense of co-relation and logic and thence developed creativity. The intelligent being in the process had begun thinking.

We need not repeat the theory or process of evolution any further here. It would be sufficient to say that as intelligence and consciousness about life and its environment developed, the survival instinct became the basic criterion of human perception. Not only this instinct of survival and feeling of insecurity also fundamentally moulded our physical bearing and behaviour but our entire psychology. Our fears and desires, likes and dislikes, in fact all our emotions have their roots in that primeval spirit.

These fears and emotions arose out of man's consciousness and apprehension of his own chances of survival in a world that was then mysterious and unknown to him. There were mysteries like the sun, the moon, the rains and the clouds. And there was death which seemed so inexplicable and yet so certain, so inevitable. It scared man and the whole world appeared to be a mystery.

There were other mysteries, other eternally esoteric questions as well :-

- How this world was created, who created this, and why ?
- Are there any purpose of this creation and of life?

- Is there any system, any logic behind the working of this creation ?
- What is death, why it is so, and is there any thing beyond it ?
- Where does the individual stand in this scheme of things ?

And then was the question of how to survive, how to be more safe and secure. These questions have always haunted the human mind. The entire development of human thought, the sciences and the arts have been directly or indirectly, an endeavour to find answers to these questions. Since no naturally apparent and convincing answer to these questions was ever available, man has always thought about and tried to answer them in different ways in every civilisation.

Anything which is beyond our comprehension affects us adversely. Enigmas seem to attack us. We are not comfortable with the unknown. It makes as feel insecure. The instinct to survive made it necessary for man to find solutions because without explanations he could not come to terms with his own existence and with his surroundings. And man was a thinking being. As a living being he had the same nature, the same desire, the same fundamental instinct as any other living being had, be it a plant or an animal. That was the instinct to survive, to perpetuate his existence. To understand and to come to terms with what was around us was thus a logical corollary of this instinctive pursuit.

Origin of God

This pursuit of survival led to the development of human knowledge and intelligence in different directions. Certain of these fields of knowledge branched out and became pure sciences. On the other hand, thinkers and philosophers tried to find their own answers by meditation, logic, or by imagining what they felt was extraterrestrial/divine revelation. These different quests led to the development of philosophies and thence to religious beliefs. As such philosophy was an outcome of a psychological necessity of the human mind. We can even say that philosophy is rationalised and elevated psychology.

So came the sages with their theories of divine origin and divine intervention. And then came the concepts of gods and prophets which became popular and were accepted primarily because there was no other satisfactory answers to the questions that mystified human mind. Belief in divinity satisfied a very basic need of human curiosity and bewilderment. We must remember that the process of survival was a very ruthless one. Only the strongest survived. There was no democracy at that time, and no concept of social justice to save the unfit. The concept of god, as a still superior being who would rescue the weak and bring help and justice to all was indeed a fascinating idea. In fact the concept of God can be regarded as the most sublime creation of the collective human mind.

Such beliefs had social and political utility as well. The codification of social order was made to derive a legitimacy through insinuation of divine origin in many societies. The structure and value system of beliefs developed differently in different societies depending on the local conditions and compulsions of their survival strategy. Thus evolved the various schools of thought (religions), some of which were to later take up the shape of religions.

Certain of these schools became so dogmatic that they made any digression a sacrilege. They put an end to the thinking process and pursued only the code of personal and social behaviour and ended up in stipulated rituals. In certain areas the system of political power drew legitimacy through halofication of the so-called divinely revealed ideas. Even today all autocratic and repressive regimes sanctify, in fact glorify divine irrationality. They perpetuate their reign of persecution and oppression in the name of some theocracy or the other, which has no basis of reason or scientific logic. In the name of God's will and decree, man has often tried to enslave and degrade and suppress another man, rather humanity itself.

Even as the theories of divine intervention, in one form or the other, gained ground across the globe, it did not convince everyone. Even long back there were skeptics and the rationalists who were not convinced about some god creating all this. To these rationalists, often pejoratively called the agnostics or the atheists, such theories did not provide a satisfactory answer, at least not all the answers. To them the divine theories opened more questions than they answered. Whereas certain societies tolerated such intellectual debates, certain other societies did not permit what was labeled as heresy. To some dogmatic adherence to ignorance gave a sense of unity and thus security, while curiosity made them feel vulnerable.

Philosophical Developments in India

Thousands of years back the land extending from the river Sindhu (Indus), and its tributaries to the foothills of Himalayas was becoming an arena of enlightened intellectual exploration. Healthy debates on all issues were being encouraged by the society. People were thinking, and debating upon not only the fundamental questions mentioned earlier but also on questions about man's relationship to nature and the other way round. This intellectualism led to development of various schools of thought and philosophies. People of this area were later to be labeled as Hindus and the philosophies they developed, even though diverse they were, were grouped together and called as the philosophy of Hinduism, although no such thing as Hinduism was ever founded or propagated. It would be technically more accurate to call these philosophies as thoughts of ancient Indian civilisation.

This development of philosophy was through several stages. The first stage was of the Rig-Veda period. Then followed three other Vedas, viz, Sama-Veda, Yajura-Veda and Atharva-Veda. This is also called the Vedic age. Many different schools came up in the post Vedic era. This was the age of Vedanta, when Upanishads and other philosophical/religious treatises were written. Gita is regarded as the culmination in this process of development of the various schools of philosophy of that time.

Gita is also the confluence point of the different streams of philosophy. It has to be remembered that this development was a sort of intellectual evolution of thought, lasting over a few thousand years and spread over a very large area. It was never one school of thought, but several centres of learning and meditation, which deliberated over the fundamental questions of life. These schools not only dealt with different areas of philosophy but at times also adopted contradictory and divergent positions on certain issues.

In Gita we find not only assimilation but also reconciliation between these varying and disparate lines of thought. The beauty lies in the fact that Gita not only contains the essence of the various philosophical tenets of the time but also puts them into a cogent and comprehensive structure. It puts the fundamentals of Indian philosophy succinctly as also provides it with practical value which can be of use to an individual in his day-to-day life. It is for this reason that Gita is called the microcosm of Indian philosophy.

The development of Indian philosophy is too elaborate a subject to be dealt here. It would suffice to have a brief overview of its various stages. For this we will take up two of the Vedas, viz., the Rig-Veda and the Atharva-Veda and some of the important Upanishads in the coming chapters.

the self. It is the inner self, a part of the all supreme *Brahm*, eternally pure, integrating with which a person attains the status of *Brahma*. It also says that a

man becomes as he acts. As such it is important that one controls oneself and takes himself to the path of

Mundaka Upanishad

2

VEDAS AND GITA

Rig-Veda

Rig-Veda is the most ancient collection of literature in the world. Archaeological evidence to indicate the period of Vedas is not conclusively available. It is estimated that Rig-Veda was composed around 2500 BC and last of the Vedas around 1000 BC. To the religious minded people however, it is traditionally regarded as the word of God, eternal and everlasting, the final word of wisdom. Historically it is associated with the ancient Aryan culture in India and is presumed to be the first of the four Vedas.

For ages Vedas remained in form of hymns/lyrics which the Aryans passed on from generation to generation, perhaps in the form of folklore, possibly with additions at various stages, incorporating the thoughts and events as they occurred. Their compilation as one epic was a much later activity.

Rig-Veda primarily gives us a beautiful insight into the Aryan society and times. The Vedic era was of a primarily agrarian society. Farming and animal husbandry were the main sources of livelihood. Trade was also fairly common. The system of administration was rudimentary and the kings were primarily warlords who kept waging wars with forest tribes as the Aryans moved eastwards for settlement.

We must remember that those were tumultuous times. We need not go into any detail or controversy now over a settlement that took place thousands of years back. It would be enough to know that the Aryans had to consistently keep struggling as they moved from the Indus valley towards the Gangetic plains. The Rig-Veda is full of panegyrics, eulogizing the lords who fought, defeated and slew the enemies. Rig-Veda has history, mythology, hymns, and philosophy. It thus gives us a first hand account of the Vedic era civilisation as such rather than of mere philosophy.

However we do find elementary traces of some philosophical thoughts which were the seeds of what were later to develop into profound philosophical concepts in the era of the Upanishads, the Vedanta age.

The concept of religion as such did not exist at that time, but there was a strong feeling of fraternal identity among the Aryans as a clan. Sacrifice was an important feature of their socio-religious lives. Ethics were high in social nature and moral values. However there never was any formal codification of the social system. People were clear about what was right and what was not, what was to be done in social behavior and what was not to be done, as a tradition. That was the *Dharma*. That is what a civilisation ought to be, orderly without a formal order.

It would be interesting to have a brief glimpse of some of those traces which are relevant to the philosophy of Bhagavad Gita, or otherwise. Some of such verses of Rig-Veda are given below :

Those brave men who die in battle are sent to heaven by lord Indra. Battle is a selfless path to heaven. (1/132/2)

When non-material nature took over the material world then who saw the first born ? Life and blood originated from the earth but from where did the soul come? (1/164/4)

Deathless soul lives with the mortal body. People understand the mortal body but not the eternal soul. (1/164/38)

Those inspired by the sun do actions as a duty. (7/63/4)

O Agni ! When the dead person goes up after cremation, encourage him to go to his ancestors. May he again attain a body. (10/16/5)

O widows of the dead man ! Think of your sons and of your house and get up from here. Why are you sleeping here. You have done your duty of marrying and bearing his children. Give up the idea of dying with him. (10/18/8)

The sage thought, 'All the animals on this earth are my images. Every man who eats food is no different from me. The Brahma who prevails over the earth and the sky is me only. (10/27/9)

O Indra ! Your expansion and the arduous tasks you did were only an illusion. All your battles were also an illusion. As you have no enemy now how did you have any in the ancient age? (10/54/2)

You are one part fire, second air and third the radiant soul. (10/56/1)

Before the origin of gods, matter originated from non-matter. Thence originated the dimensions and then the plant life. (10/72/3)

Whatever has occurred and whatever is to occur is only the viraat purusha. He is the lord of being as he leaves the causation state and enters into the matter state. All living beings get sustenance from him. (10/90/2)

This expansion of universe originated from the primeval man. He made land and from earth was created life. (10/90/5)

In the state of flood / flux (beginning) there was neither matter nor non-matter neither being nor non-being. At that time there was neither the world nor the space (neither the sky nor anything beyond). There was neither life anywhere nor any source of pleasure. What was there ? And where ? What was the power ? At that time even the solemn water was not existing. (10/129/1)

At that time there was neither death nor immortality. There was neither the night nor the notion of day. At that time only one (Brahma), imbued with life energy in his nature, breathed, and nothing else existed. (10/129/2)

It was all darkness everywhere (darkness hidden in darkness) and the existence was unknown (was formless and fluid). With tapas, self exertion (power of heat), out of nothingness (void) emerged Brahma, without external cause or action. (10/129/3)

This caused the conception of creation of the universe. It formed the seed of the entire creation. The sages thought over this and found cause of matter out of non-matter. (10/129/4)

Who knows the entire truth and who can speak about this creation ? What were the causative factors of this creation ? The gods have originated after the creation . Who knows the one from which this world has got created? (10/129/6)

It is unknown how this existence has come up. He only knows, the one who created this or unveiled it. Does he bear it or not ? It is unknown whether the lord up above knows it or not? (10/129/7)

What is the proof of the time when gods organised the yagna of prajapati ? What was the image of god at that time? What were the offerings and the chants? (10/130/3)

In Rig-Veda we find mention of a very large number of gods, venerated for their superhuman/ preternatural powers, like Indra. However this should not be confused as polytheism. The gods mentioned still fall short of absolute divinity. None of them is unqualified the Supreme Being or the Creator. Many of them were functional gods, like a god for rain, one for fire and another one for some other function. Even among the pantheon of gods, or lords described, the hierarchy is not well defined, as it is understood now.

Some of these gods were perhaps outstanding historical figures and divine attributes got associated with them in time and legend, out of esteem and awe. They were mostly figures who fought for the Aryans and did well at that. Verses in their praise are mostly by way of eulogy. These verses are good poetry but with little or no philosophical content in them.

However the really important and unique concept of a supreme all pervading power, *Brahma,* as the material and efficient cause of existence had started emerging in the Rig-Veda. In no other civilisation or philosophy do we have such a concept, which is on one hand transcendental in metaphysical attributes yet on the other hand, comes closest to anticipating the modern scientific theories of creation. We will discuss the concept of *Brahma* later while discussing the Upanishads, for it was in the age of Vedanta when the sages in great detail discussed the concept of *Brahma*.

Belief in the concept of soul as something immortal was getting stronger at that time. It appears to have been a concept that predated the Vedic age. Similarly, belief in after life and in transmigration of soul (rebirth) was also fairly prevalent. These concepts of soul, and the theory of transmigration were also discussed in Gita, though the philosophy of Gita is not based on the assumption of immortality of soul as we understand soul. This subject is also dealt in greater detail later.

The concept of selfless action, which became a dominant theme in Gita is also mentioned in Rig-Veda, though only in a few sporadic places.

Rig-Veda has no magic *mantras*. There is nothing to support existence of superstition or dogma in the Vedic society.

It is also to be noticed that some of the compositions of Rig-Veda are agnostic in outlook. They indicate an open mind in questioning the cause and reason of existence and creation. They even question about the creator! It appears that at that time no definite or conclusive theory on the concept of God or the creator had been propagated, or accepted conclusively by the society, and there was a profound desire to find answers to these fundamental questions.

One has to understand and accept that Vedas were not compositions of a single individual but form the collective thought of a community, and as such doubts, digressions and contradictions were unavoidable. In fact it was the presence of these debatable issues, which made further probe in the philosophical areas imperative. This provided a fertile ground for intellectual debates/thoughts to prosper and consequently led to further development of various schools of philosophy and metaphysics in India.

The entire intellectual activity of the period of Rig-Veda thus provided the basis of the Indian/ Hinduism, philosophy and culture.

Atharva-Veda

Like Rig-Veda, the Atharva- Veda also deals with a whole gamut of themes of the Aryan society. Here we will briefly discuss only the philosophical aspects dealt in it, particularly the ones that were to be further developed in Gita.

In Atharva-Veda we find less of skepticism, noticed frequently in the Rig-Veda. The tenor is more authoritative and statements are made with firmness of conviction. Many of the concepts of Rig-Veda are seen developed further and in a more formalised manner.

The most important of these was the concept of *Brahma*. This *Brahma* is also known as *ohm* (in sound form). In no sense can *Brahma* be compared with God, as we understand/conceptualise God. *Brahma* is not something like a superman who created the world, who thinks and watches like the big brother, who keeps an account of the good and the evil, and dispenses justice like a phantom. In fact *Brahma* does nothing by way of action: *Brahma* is the cause of actions taking place.

Brahma is the energy as well as the cause of the energy of creation. He is timeless. He has always existed, in form of energy, without shape or form, and he created the world out of himself, out of nothing (void), of his own volition, for the joy of creating. He is omnipresent, all pervading, immanent in everything in existence, and the cause as well as the source of everything.

Here we will have just a few samples of Atharva-Veda which may be of interest and relevance to the context. (These are translations of only part of the verses.)

He has many forms, and although He is known by many names He is one. (9/16/28)

Brahma is without desire, without attachment, and is self actuated. (10/8 /44)

He is living as well as the non-living, He is being and the non-being as well. (13/4/19)

The concept of *Brahma* had become much more important and elaborate in Atharva Veda. The concept had become clearer, more metaphysical and was later in the Vedanta age to become almost the central theme of the Upanishads.

It is interesting to note that concepts like life originating from non-living, matter originating from non-matter and convertibility of energy into matter, which now stand the test of modern science were emphatically propounded in Vedas as divine truth. However in the Vedas, and later in the Upanishads these concepts were proposed not by way of any scientific theory on the origin of life but to help man in establishing his own identity in the existence and to establish a unison and harmony with the nature. It was a prime concept, and concern of the philosophers of that time was that all the apparent appearances, understandable by senses, were manifestations of one, i.e., *Brahma*, and so the individual should not consider himself distinct or different either from other individuals or from his environment/nature. The emphasis was to establish a synthesis among the various forms of manifestations of *Brahma*.

Another concept, which had further gained firm ground, was of the immortality of soul. The verses 8/1/8 & 9 say- *The dead was not to be grieved for*. This was to become a dominant theme in Gita. When Arjuna decides not to fight in the battle out of his attachment for his kinsmen Krishna tells Arjuna that he need not grieve for the dead as the soul is immortal. However, in Gita immortality of soul is not the basis of the entire logic and in fact Krishna also tells Arjuna that even if he does not believe in soul, he still should not shirk from his righteous duties as a warrior because death is in any case inevitable.

The theory of reincarnation according to the nature and deeds of a person on earth is also sustained in Atharva-Veda. This concept is dealt very differently in Gita. Although the concepts of soul and of rebirth have been discussed, and upheld in Gita, they are neither the central logic of Gita, nor is the soul as dealt in Gita the same in concept as we tend to understand it normally. Soul is treated almost as analogous to a metaphysical inner 'Self', a quantity that transcends consciousness. We will discuss the theme later on the concerned subject.

The thinkers of the Vedic age thus made most significant contribution in the development of Indian philosophy by raising issues of fundamental importance and attempting their answers.

3

UPANISHADS AND GITA

Upanishad's literally means is secret teachings. The Upanishads are about 110 in number and they embody the cream of Vedic thought. They are mostly a part of some larger epic (just as Gita is a part of Mahabharata). Having been composed at the later stages of the Vedic era they are also known as the Vedanta. They do not deal with mythology or ritualism. These are philosophical treatises. They deal with various themes, often overlapping and sometimes mutually contradicting. They represent the different schools of thought of the time.

It is said that the Vedic period at one time was becoming too ritualistic, and the development of thought had become stagnant. In a sense the period of Upanishads represents a renaissance in the development of Hindu philosophy. It was in this age that foundations of Hindu thought were laid on firm philosophical grounds. Later developments were superstructures, and also aberrations, of this foundation. In another sense they were also a reaction from the ritualistic customs which had developed in the later Aryan society. Upanishads emphasised on thought and meditation and developed the basic metaphysics of the Indian philosophy.

Some of the fundamental concepts of Indian philosophy took firm shape in the Upanishads. The most significant of these was the development of the concept of *Brahma*.

Concept of Brahma

Some of the Upanishads say that it is impossible to explain *Brahma* by words, nor is it possible to understand it by intellect. You cannot know *Brahma* by way of reasoning. Then how do we understand what is *Brahma* ?

The Vedic scholars treated *Brahma* as the source of creation, not as the conscious creator. *Brahma* is not a creator in the sense that He was a powerful and conscious being who existed before the existence of the universe. *Brahma* was something from which the existence came out into being. *Brahma* was an entity possessed only with heat energy but was without consciousness or desires. Creation occurred out of *Brahma*, not by *Brahma*, and it occurred out of non-matter and without any external cause.

The scientific theory on the phenomenon of creation says that in the beginning the entire universe was condensed in the form of a black hole. It was all dark and nothing existed, as described in the Veda. Then occurred an explosion, the big bang. To quote Stephen Hawking from his book *A Brief History of Time*- 'At the big bang, the universe is thought to have had zero size and so to have been infinitely hot.' (Recall the word *tapas* of the earlier quote of Rig-Veda. *Tap* is heat.) This explosion led to creation of this universe and from then on the universe is continuously expanding.

Brahma is not the god in the traditional sense. It is not something away or superior to the living beings either. Instead we all are a part of a common source of the eternal cause which is *Brahma*. Although we use the pronoun 'He' for *Brahma* out of reverence, one should not confuse it with a living god. Alternative use of impersonal pronoun 'it' for *Brahma* can also be done without any offense. To understand *Brahma* we have to understand ourselves, and where we stand, with a steady and detached mind.

If we are swayed by the yearnings of our senses, by our desires and cravings, then we lose our power of discernment. We then get lost within ourselves, with what is superficial, and thus fail to perceive what is beyond, what is the ultimate, the true, and the absolute. Discernment is the power to see things in absolute terms, unconnected with anything that is us, or with anything that we consider as ours.

The concept of *Brahma* was further elaborated in Atharva-Veda, and in the Vedanta, i.e., in Upanishads it was the main subject of thought. The main characteristics of *Brahma* as described in Vedanta are :-

1. *Brahma* is *nirguna*, it does not have any material qualities.
2. *Brahma* is neither living nor non-living, or is both. It is formless. It is material as well as non-material.
3. *Brahma* is not conscious in the way we understand a conscious being. He is neither a person nor he takes decisions.

We should have control over ourselves and try to establish unity and harmony with the entire system, which is beyond our control or understanding. This requires an equanimous system of perception which can be attained by knowledgeable, practice of thinking (meditation) and/or by performance of detached actions.

These are the ways of integrating oneself with *Brahma* (*yoga*) which is the only way of knowing *Brahma*.

It would not only be impossible but also unfair to try to squeeze the philosophy of Upanishads into a few pages. With apologies, here we will have a cursory look at some of the verses of a few Upanishads and discuss the concepts/subjects related to the philosophy of Gita.

Isha-Vasya-Upanishad

Ohm purnamadah purnamidam purnat purnamudchyate
purnasya purnamadaya purnamevavashishyate

Ohm (Brahma) is complete in all respects. This existence is also complete, having originated from completeness. Completeness still remains after complete is taken out of completeness.

Isha vasyamidam sarvam yatikinch jagatyam jagat
tain tyaktain bhunjitha ma gradah kasya svid dhanam (1)

Whatever exists in the universe is pervaded with God. Keeping God with self, enjoy the existence with abandonment, do not get attached. To whom can the worldly treasures belong.

Kurvanneveh karmani jijivishechchhatam samah
evam tvayi nanyatheto asti na karma lipyate nare (2)

Performing works only as a prayer to God, wish to live for a period of hundred years. Works so done do not get attached to the man. There is no other way for salvation.

Isha-vasya Upanishad is the briefest of the Upanishads but it deals with two extremely important concepts, i.e., *Brahma* and detachment. These concepts were to be dealt in much greater detail in Gita and were to be its central theme. The beauty lies in the way the two have been rationally inter-linked in this Upanishad. That is why it is considered as foremost among the Upanishads.

Isha-vasya Upanishad opens with the statement that *Brahma* is complete in himself. From this completeness the existence has come into being and still *Brahma* remains complete. It may have different forms, that is to say, the energy-matter changes forms, but it cannot be lost from the total system. *Brahma* is within everything and yet outside everything. Thus we, and all that we sense through our sensory faculties, and what is beyond us and our sensory faculties is *Brahma*.

We all are a part of this *Brahma* (system of existence), which is dynamic and interchangeable.

Next it states that whatever material things exist belong to the existence. They cannot be taken anywhere (out of this completeness of *Brahma*) and hence they cannot be the possession of any individual. The material possessions are like temporary facilities to us. We may use/enjoy/consume them but should not be attached to them, or covet them, because as mortal beings have to leave them behind one day.

Once we realise our unity and harmony with *Brahma*, of which we are a part, then there is no distinction between the individuals (since all are part of the *Brahma*) and also there is no need for attachment to possessions (because nothing really belongs to us). As such we need not covet earthly things.

Hence it may be natural to overcome fear of loss of life or worldly possessions because these are in any case are not to be with us forever. They are not our eternal possessions but temporary facilities. It also makes feelings of greed or hatred illogical and short sighted.

One who sees god/*Brahma* in everything, including himself, hates no one as he identifies himself and others as a part of the all encompassing *Brahma*. In fact he becomes *Brahma*. To become *Brahma* is to merge oneself into the infinite eternal being, lose all sense of ego, of selfness, of separate individuality. This is a release from mere mortal existence, rather a liberation from the existence. It is a state of mind, and has little to do with outward appearances. Once reached that state, then one is not attached to anything.

Further, if we are not physically attached to things then we also do not get affected by our works/actions also as they do not get linked to us. Thus we get rid of the ego of being the doer. This concept of being (considering oneself as) the non-doer even while doing the works becomes the central theme of Gita. The pure and unattached self becomes everything and there is internal peace and equanimity in the 'self' while the body keeps doing the necessary functions. This knowledge of being a non-doer in fact must get reflected in our actions, and peace is obtained through such detached actions.

In Gita we read Shri Krishna repeatedly telling Arjuna how a person can attain the supreme state of integrating himself with *Brahma*, i.e., of becoming *Brahma*. As *Brahma* is the Supreme, eternal and imperishable one, this concept of a human being attaining the divine like attributes was not only something new but unique to the Hindu philosophy where the man is not considered as something low and degradable as such. The human being, as per Hindu philosophy has the capability/choice of elevating/transcending himself to the supreme state, by means of *yoga*, devotion, etc., Whether one does it or not is another matter.

Kena-Upanishad

Yanamanasa na manute yenahurmano matam
tadev brahma tvam vidhi nedam yadidmupasate (I - 5)

What cannot be understood by intellect, instead what provides understanding to the intellect, that should be known as Brahma. What is worshipped by mind and intellect is not Brahma.

Both Kena-Upanishad and ***Mandukya-Upanishad*** explain that *Brahma* is everything as well as the cause of everything. *Brahma* cannot be seen, heard or understood because it/He is the cause (and the source of energy) behind sight, intellect (understanding) and life itself. That is to say *Brahma* is beyond the grasp of sensory faculties because it is the cause of functioning/existence of the sensory faculties. He (*Brahma*) can be known only by the spirit/soul (inner self).

It may be worth while to clarify here itself that in the Indian philosophical parlance, mind and intellect are also considered as sensory faculties. They are only just a step higher in the hierarchy of senses, e.g., the intellect can discriminate and can control the mind as well as the senses. But it is not away from the sensory faculties of the body. And all these faculties form the part of the body. So when we talk of the body, the sensory faculties like the power of hearing, the power of understanding, etc., get included automatically.

Katha-Upanishad

Yastu vigyanvan bhavati samanaskah sada shuchi
sa tu tatpadamaproti yasmad bhuyo na jayate (I/3/8)

He who is of discerning mind, self controlled and pure, he attains the supreme status, and is not born again.

Paranchi khani vyatranat svayambhu stasmatparangam pashyati nantaratman
kashchiddhirah pratyagatmanmaiksh davratt chakshur amratavam ichchan (2/1/1)

Creator made all the senses to open outwards. So man looks only externally, and not towards his own soul. Only some wise person, desirous of the supreme state, reverses his senses from external objects and looks at his soul.

Yada sarve pramuchyante kama ye asya hradi shritah
ath martyo amrato bhavatyatra brahma samshrute (2/3/14)

When all the desires are totally destroyed then the mortal man becomes immortal and experiences Brahma here itself.

Katha-Upanishad fundamentally deals with the concept of soul. It says that soul is pure and it is beyond reasoning. Soul is unaffected by the works of the individual. Soul transmigrates due to the cycle of rebirths. Deeds of the previous life affect the next life. *Moksha* is release from this cycle of rebirths. For this release one has to merge his senses into mind, mind into knowledge, knowledge into self, self into the pure soul and soul into the god. Our senses are windows to look out. Man tends to look only outside but the need is to look inside oneself (objective introspection). This is possible only with a steady, unaffected and a mind without desires.

The concepts of this Upanishad though do not form the basis of the logic of Gita, yet some of these concepts were used in a very subtle and sublime form. Whereas Krishna tells Arjuna that one should not grieve for the dead as the soul is immortal, he also says that in case Arjuna does not believe in the phenomenon of immortality of soul, there is still no reason for grieving, as death is in any case unavoidable, and what is inevitable need not be lamented about.

The concepts of soul and of rebirth though upheld in Gita are treated very differently, as we shall see later in the concerned chapter. Other concepts of this Upanishad are also seen only very scantily in Gita although some of these were later to become an important stream of thought in the socio-religious ethos of the Indian society.

Brahad-Aranyaka- Upanishad

Ath karmana atmam aitye tadresha mukthamato hi sarvani karmanyuttishthnye yadesham samaitadhi sarvaih karmabhih samametadesham prahamaitdhi sarvani karmani vibhati (1/6/3)

Soul is the material cause of all action because it originates all actions. And as soul bears all the works it is also the Brahma.

Brihad-Aranyaka-Upanishad says that gods forsake the man who thinks of world/god other than the self. It is the inner self, a part of the all supreme *Brahma*, eternally pure, integrating with which a person attains the status of *Brahma*. It also says that a man becomes as he acts. As such it is important that one controls oneself and takes himself to the path of salvation. It is beautifully said in Gita that man is his best friend and his own worst enemy. If he decides to elevate himself to a higher level, towards the state of *Brahma*, he becomes his own friend. But if he does not control himself and degrades himself, he becomes his own enemy.

It is through action that one reaches to attainment of the state of *Brahma*. This is further elaborated in Gita by stressing the importance of performing actions (finding happiness in the excellence of one's actions rather than in the results), which are dutiful, and in accordance to ones' nature.

Mundaka-Upanishad

Nayamatma pravachnen labhyo na medhaya na bahuna shruten
yamevaish vranute ten labhyastasyaish atma vivranute tanum svam (3/2/3)

Brahma is not achieved either by sermons nor by intellect or by words. Whom Brahma accepts to him it reveals its manifest form.

Sa yo ha vai tatparamam brahma veda brahmaiva bhavati
nasya brahma vitkule bhavati
tarati shokam tarati papmanam guhagranthibhyo vimukto
amrato bhavati (3/2/9)

He who gets to know Brahma becomes Brahma himself. No one remains unaware of Brahma in his family. He transcends grief and all the sins. Relieved of all complexes, he becomes immortal.

Mundaka-Upanishad emphasizes that it is not by penance or rituals that one can understand *Brahma*. Gita is in fact extremely critical of the physical tortures that certain people inflict on themselves with the hope sof attaining the supreme. Gita similarly views mere outward following of rituals as of little value. What is emphasised in Gita is the mental outlook and personal conduct, which are important in attaining the supreme, not the superficial appearances.

He who understands *Brahma*, by self realisation/ actualisation becomes *Brahma* himself and is relieved of pain and guilt/sin. He thus becomes virtually immortal, as he takes no cognisance of death as something different from life. And so, Krishna says in Gita, Arjuna should fight in the battle without fear or guilt of death or of killing his Kinsmen.

Shvetashvatara-Upanishad

Gyagyo dvavajaveesh nisha vaja hyoka bhotra bhogyartha yukta
anantsh cha atma vishvarupo hyakarta trayam yada vindate brahmametat (1/1/9)

Omniscient and omnipotent (god) and ignorant and incapable (conscious life force) are both immortal. Nature, which provides all that is consumed by the life is the third eternal and immortal force. As the supreme is of infinite forms and devoid of the ego of being the doer, when man so realises god life and nature as a form of Brahma, he finds liberation.

Shvetashvatara-Upanishad deliberates upon some of the important issues discussed earlier in the other Upanishads and later in Gita also.

This Upanishad postulates that God is free from selfishness or bias in his actions, as he is not attached. Feelings of 'I' and 'Mine' are outcome of selfish desires and confusion. In fact such feelings basically arise out of ignorance about the world system. These feelings do not lead the individual to peace of mind because the person filled with desires and expectations depends on external fulfillment for peace and happiness.

The soul (inner self) can find real and lasting peace only within its own sources, not from outside. Man becomes what he thinks. Mind is the source of liberation as well as of bondage, because everything is the way we look at it. Ego and pride of being the doer is due to not discovering of the unity of man with god/nature. This integration alone can bring salvation and peace of mind.

Nature, and thus body, is perishable. The soul/self, which utilises body as a mere facility for executing works, is immortal. Man should be free of illusions and watch the processes of life as a witness and not be a mere consumer/owner. It is the consumer who is bound by the products. Liberation is freedom from such bonds of external sustenance of peace and happiness.

The basic idea of this Upanishad is also that detachment is the only way of internal liberation and hence of peace of mind. It also clarifies that it is possible for the individual to uplift himself from a mere mortal life of physical attachments and to find liberation in this world itself. Man's conscious behaviour is an enactment of his sub-conscious image of himself. He can seek integration with *Brahma* and thus transcend his own self to a higher plane and thus liberate himself from the bondages, which are self assumed. It all depends how a person decides to think. That is why control over mind is so important.

Shvetashvatara-Upanishad also proposed the concept of the Wheel of creation, the *Wheel of Brahma/ Brahma Chakra* (eternal and indestructible time which ruthlessly always keeps moving). It also discussed the idea of *Maya,* the power of wonder or the power of creation of God.

For these concepts, this Upanishad is also considered among the most important of the Upanishads.

Maitri-Upanishad deals on the similar theme of *Brahma.* It says that only a confused mind thinks of the 'self ' as a separate being. The individual is part of the larger cosmic order, i.e., the *Brahma.* It is imperative for mental peace that one synthesizes oneself with what is other than him. *Yoga* is this integration of the self with the *Brahma. Yoga* is the establishment of harmony with the entire existence, the process of creating oneness with nature/*Brahma.* With such harmony established, path of man's salvation / liberation is clear.

Moksha is the liberation from rebirths. It is not something achieved after death but a release on this earth itself. It is the freedom from ego of self-consciousness. Mind is the cause of bondage as well as of release. It depends on attachment. Once the feeling of detachment is aroused everything appears different. It is a state of sort of mindlessness, where mind is unattached, unclinging and undistracted, on a transcended and different plane.

Maitri-Upanishad also propounded the concept of indestructibility of time and space. *Brahma* is not bound by time and is beyond all logic/thought. In Gita, Krishna tells Arjuna that it is impossible to understand the divine by logic. There are mysteries, which cannot be known.

Chandogya-Upanishad says that if man is ruled by the body and senses then he is in bondage. If he is ruled by the spirit then he is free. This Upanishad also treats mind as just another organ, the organ of thought, one of the faculties of the physical body. This concept is used for getting rid of ego and allied complexes as we often take responsibility and hence guilt for what is done by mind though feel we are not that responsible for the developments of the body. These two concepts, i.e., need of control over the senses and of mind being as another one of those sensory faculties are further discussed in Gita.

Taittiriya-Upanishad

So akamayat, bahu syam prajayeyeti, sa tapo atapyat, sa tapastaptva idam sarvam rajat yadidam kim cha, tatsrashtva tadevanu pravishat, tadanu pravishya sachch tyachchabhavat, niruktam chaniruktam cha, nilyanam chanilyanam cha, vigyanam cha avigyanam cha, satyam chanratam cha satyam bhavata, yadidam kim cha, tatsatya mitya chakshate (2/6)

He (Supreme Brahma) thought I must manifest myself and prevail/pervade. So resolved he created the existence we see. Having created he entered the same existence and became material as well as abstract, describable as well as indescribable, living as well as non-living. Truth and untruth was also him. Whatever can be seen or experienced is true.

Besides the above discussed nine Upanishads, *Taittiriya, Aitreya* and *Prashna* Upanishads also deal with somewhat similar subjects and are considered important among the Upanishads dealing with philosophical readings.

There are other Upanishads which deal with subjects like the physical ways of practicing *yoga,* austerity, renunciation (*sanyas*), etc., which need no discussion here.

It is difficult to summarise the philosophies of the Upanishads in brief. However we can say that Upanishads tried to answer some of the fundamental questions raised in the Vedic age.

The above exploration of some of the important Upanishads was just an attempt to have a general idea of the concepts/theories and of the schools of philosophical thinking which had already preceded Gita, which were already under discussion at the time of Mahabharata. We find that many of the concepts dealt in Gita already existed before Mahabharata was composed.

As said earlier, the beauty of Gita lies in the way these various concepts were linked into a wholesome composite and rational philosophy. Gita ironed out the rise of ritualism, cautioned against aberrations that had cropped up in the society and gave emphasis to rational thinking. In a way it was a great philosophical correction in the culture of that time.

Further and more significantly, the entire package was not just for meditation or intellectual entertainment (satisfaction) : it had, and has, in present times more than ever before, immense practical value.

4

OBJECTIVES OF GITA

What exactly is Gita ? What is that practical value mentioned so much about it ? Why Gita was composed in the particular context in the Mahabharata and what were the objectives behind the philosophy of Gita ?

We will now try to answers of these questions before we go into the important philosophical concepts of Gita.

The discourse of Bhagavad Gita opens up with Arjuna's profound dilemma-to fight or not to fight ? He had to decide upon questions of great importance-To kill or to restrain ? To usurp or to abdicate ? What is wrong and what is right ? Who is to decide upon these questions ? And why ?

Answers of these questions are not simple at any time. They involve the human psychology in its entire situation. Arjuna is in a dilemma only because of the peculiar situation in which he finds himself. Without that situation there would be no need for any mental confusion to arise in the mind of Arjuna. But Arjuna is also not responsible for the situation that has come up. And he is averse to the only solution offered to him, rather available to him, which is to fight against and kill his own relatives. He is averse to this course of action because of his value system.

Arjuna, like all of us, is a product of his situation and his dilemma is but a manifestation of the contradictions within his value system when placed in a situation for which his value system is not fully prepared (programmed).

Krishna tells Arjuna that he finds himself in this state of indecision, in a state of dilemma only because of the way he perceives his situation. His confusion is a result of his own preset premises, which are misplaced. These contradictions and confusions in Arjuna's mind are of his own making and belief. They are his individual/personal predicaments and not universal problems. They are also merely contextual. But Arjuna should not take an individualistic view if he is to solve his contradictions for good. He has to take an overall, a holistic view of life. He has to review his value system in the context of the all pervading situation. He has to introspect, identify his own place in the total cosmic system, and understand how the system works, and then decide his course of action. The discourse of Gita helps man to do this.

Self Realisation

Gita as a treatise of philosophy stands unique in this respect as it involves the reader into an intense brainstorming, without sermonising and without ever divorcing from the practical aspects of an individual's life in society. The objective is not to provide man with a ready-made methodology or solution. Gita does not give the individual an aim but the idea is to enable the individual to identify himself in the system, decide upon his options, determine his aims and pursue them. The objective is to help him think logically and rationally so that he is clear about himself and also of his aims and objectives in life.

Gita does not propagate any religion nor does it espouse the cause of any god. It is not a book of social morality either. Gita preaches no rituals, it sets no dogmas, and lays down no code of personal or social behaviour. Far from binding man into any type of guideline, it sets the mind free to think logically and rationally so that man is able to introspect and thus find his own answers, according to his own nature and situation.

Individuals differ in various ways. They differ in terms of intelligence, in terms of nature (psychology), in physical terms and in situational terms. Of course these factors also interact and affect each other. Since no two individuals can be in exactly the same physical and mental situation there cannot be a general solution for everyone. One has to find his own solutions, depending on his nature and his situation. And so Gita instead of providing a general solution helps the individual to find his solution.

Individuals may have to have their own ways. There is a separate way of peace for the men of knowledge and a separate way for the men of action. Man can find peace only in accordance with one's nature, not against it. And it may be better to follow the solution guided by one's own nature than to follow someone else blindly. That may give no peace or happiness. In the last chapter Krishna declares that it is better to follow one's own law, one's own nature (and conscience) than to adopt what is proposed by someone else! (XVIII-47 & 48).

Thus the objective or rather the endeavour is to make the individual understand/realise himself in the context of his nature and environment, i.e., the cosmic system of the entire creation, and thereby to make the individual to come to terms with his realities so that he attains peace of mind and is able to pursue his own course in life without doubts or confusion. Thus the peace one attains through Gita is not by some divine miracle, or by indoctrination into a faith, but by sheer rational introspection and logical conclusion. In other terms it makes one realise where exactly he stands in the cosmic system.

Objectivity in Self Assessment

Gita ordains no postulates. The aim of Gita is not to streamline the society through divine edicts. There are no preset conditions or starting beliefs or assumptions in Gita. There is no detailed moralising and in a way it does not claim to be the end of wisdom. One need not believe in any concept of any religion, or even in god, in order to understand and take benefit out of the philosophy of Gita. No hell awaits those who do not follow Gita. Gita issues no final edict and puts no blinkers. Krishna is imparting the knowledge of Gita to Arjuna only because he is a dear friend to Him.

Krishna tells Arjuna at the conclusion of the discourse that if he still is of a different opinion he has the option to follow the dictates of his own nature, because ultimately going against one's nature may not bring peace.

"I have told you the wisdom, Most mysterious of all mysteries

Think over it, And then act as you wish." (XVIII- 63)

And Arjuna is finally left free to make his own choice. There are no straight jackets. Krishna lets Arjuna to take a thoughtful decision. Gita is teaching, not indoctrination or brainwash.

Krishna further says that it is better to follow one's own law than to blindly follow the law given by someone else even if that is considered as superior. This is to say that a superficially adopted thinking is not likely to give any peace. There is not just one single way for happiness. One who is incapable of meditation can get no tranquillity by adopting the posture of meditation. If the lion tries to become a saintly goat he can get nowhere. There is a strong role of natural tendencies. Evil tendencies force one to do evil. So knowing oneself (introspection) is extremely important.

What is most important is that the individual should be able to free himself from the prejudices of his own notions/complexes (about himself) and understand himself. Only then can he discern what is good for him. Free mind is essential to understanding oneself, his basic nature. And understanding oneself, and what is occurring around us, is fundamental to resolving mental confusions. Understanding the total situation tells us of our choices, or about the lack of same. Without such understanding, and equanimity in that understanding, there can be no mental peace.

Peace of Mind

One can also say that attaining peace of mind through a steady and stable thinking system is one of the fundamental objectives of the discourse of Gita.

However this peace of mind is not suggested in a hermitage or in the mountains. Peace is obtained not just by visiting a temple or by chanting. At no stage has abdication or escapism been suggested in Gita. In fact such outwardly/physical renunciations are considered as acts of hypocrisy and cowardice, and of no value.

Sanyas (physical renunciation of the material world) adopted outwardly, without achieving complete mental detachment, is no solution. It is not the way to peace of mind. It neither helps the society nor the individual. In actual life also we find that a sizable number of *sadhus* in India are ex-convicts, fugitives and absolute drug addicts. It can hardly be said that they have achieved any peace of mind. They mostly disturb the peace of mind of others also. Their emphasis on the cosmetics of clothing and appearance indicates a facade for the lack of mental conviction.

Material renunciation is escapism and exercises of austerity (penance) alone may never give peace because it is against man's basic nature and physical requirements. It is not in the nature of any living being to lead such a life of abstinence and self denial/self mortification. It is against man's survival instinct to abstain and torture oneself. One has to be either totally intoxicated/fascinated with such an idea (masochism) or it can be an unusual trait in an individual to live such a life voluntarily and happily. It may also be sheer hypocrisy to gain attention. Either way it is unnecessary.

In any case Gita does not advocate any such thing. The discourse of Gita is not for those who have renounced the world. The individual of Gita is a man of the world, the average person we see on the streets, working to survive and live better, compelled to act, to do things due to his own nature and due to his situations. And peace of mind or mental salvation/ liberation is the need of such a man of the world, of one who lives an ordinary life in society, who has to perform the day-to-day jobs, sometimes perhaps against his grain and liking, due to practical compulsions and necessities of life.

Since the average man has to continue with such a physical life it is desirable that he comes to terms with it and attains peace while still being in the system.

Yoga

Peace of mind is achieved by the self reconciling with the world, with the creation, with this system of life and death. Peace of mind comes when a harmony and equilibrium is established with this cosmic system. This is the state of *Yoga* or mental integration. This integration is between the self and the environment, the body and the mind, the knowledge and the sensory desires. *Yoga* is ultimately the unison with *Brahma*.

The state of *Yoga* is achieved not by superstitions, rituals, physical acrobatics or by blind faith but by logic and rationalisation. By reconstructing one's thinking system, almost like programming the mind and psyche, one can place one's poise and peace of mind beyond the reach of external disturbances. The individual, with *yogic* state of mind, does not turn into a stoic or become physically inert to things material. He attains no superhuman qualities. He only starts to view things differently. He becomes immune to affectations. He does not become mentally insensitive : he becomes mentally more clear about the truth and hence is not swayed by the appearances. He develops a wider perspective, he makes a holistic assessment about realities of life and begins to give weightage to things as due, neither more nor less. He gains aplomb and poise in his perception and behaviour.

Ours is an age of action and stress both. No progress is possible without action. In fact progress has a momentum of its own which is impossible to stop. However stress, strain, conflicts and tensions are the concomitants of progress. They cannot be avoided or denied. But with a slight change of attitude they can be lived with. This change of attitude can be sustaining/convincing only if it is rational. At least not always, because the world system does not appear to be so divinely regulated at all the times.

Gita provides that rationale, that we should understand and accept this process of continuity and conflict, identify our role in this scheme of things and contribute our lot in keeping the *Wheel of Brahma* moving.

Gita and Self Management

Gita can best be described as a guide to self management. Our problems are often because we do not understand ourselves. This is the reason we are unable to manage ourselves, and we go about blaming others for such of our failures which would not have occurred in the first place had we known the situation from perspective. We try to manage situations only by trying to change everything according to our liking. But management means negotiating, and negotiating involves self repositioning also. For this knowing oneself is imperative. We have to know ourselves before we can manage ourselves. Once we are able to manage ourselves, managing the rest becomes easier. This self management is done through constant practice, the *yoga,* the exercise for integration. It is like training one's own mind.

In every field today emphasis is given on training people about various skills. Have we given our own mind, which is so supremely important, any training on how to think ? Do we keep our minds fit enough to face all situations rationally instead of being swayed by emotions, or by the compulsions of the senses ?

Education gives knowledge; learning is all about what to think. *Yoga* is training the mind about how to think. Like programming the mind. Through this training of the thinking system, various aspects of life can be rationalised and the whole philosophy can be put into action. Meditation gives us the theory of this knowledge but our actions are what makes it perfect. As such the whole world is the gymnasium for such fitness. We only have to keep ourselves under our own control, be able to reflect back and be conscious to effect into action what we think. And think what we know we should be thinking.

The objective of Gita is thus to make us think straight, so that we are able to come out of our complexes and attain peace of mind. After all we can only change our own selves, our own way of thinking. But we do not try to look at ourselves. We only look towards others, outside, which is beyond our control. And hence we remain dependent on others, anxious, expectant, perturbed and without peace.

As a total philosophy the ambit of objectives of Gita is certainly much larger and it is impossible to discuss them here as this is only an attempt to find the value of Gita to the individual of the present times.

Some of the thoughts of practical value in Gita for an individual are discussed in the Chapter 'The Yogi-Manager'

5

MAYA : THE MYSTIC SYSTEM

The philosophy of Gita is a composite philosophy and it can best be understood as a whole, in totality. It would not be desirable if the various verses of Gita are read in bits and pieces. Such part may create confusions, and may give a very contorted view of its philosophical tenets. This emphasis on only some of the tenets, or such impression based on a few verses as the philosophy of Gita may be very erroneous. In order to understand the philosophy of Gita as a whole, it is imperative that the total system is understood first.

Since the entire philosophy of Gita examines the individual in the wider context of the entire existence it would be logical to discuss the system of existence, the cosmic order, in which the individual spends his lifetime.

What is this world, this entire existence that we see around us?

What is this system in which the individual exists?

Who created this existence? How ?

And why? For what purpose?

How does it operate?

Are there any systems / procedures / laws of its ways of working?

In the earlier chapters we have already discussed that these questions had always perplexed the human mind and in different civilisations different answers were propounded. We have also gone through the theories as propagated in the Vedas and Upanishads. According to these ancient texts the entire creation was initially concealed in a condensed state which had no form or shape. That was the *Brahma,* the imperishable in dormant state, a state which was neither being nor non-being, neither matter nor non-matter, neither existent nor non-existent, a sort of form of energy. *Brahma* was then just a state, which was also expressed by the sound "*ohm*".

Brahma has always existed. From this *Brahma* , and by His own volition/desire (out of its own internal energy/dynamics) the entire existence that we see came into being. One other interpretation can be that the entire existence always existed because *Brahma* is the existence. All that happened was that *Brahma* unveiled the existence, and so it is apparent to our organs of senses now.

Science also speculates upon various such theories which propose the origin of the world somewhat on similar lines, only different, being in scientific terminology.

Although this issue of creation and creator was not immediately or directly relevant to the context in which the discourse of Gita began, it would not have been possible to skip over such an issue. Firstly, Krishna who delivers the discourse of Gita is mythologically speaking himself God Vishnu incarnate. Further, if He has to make Arjuna understand his real self, his situation in totality, and his relationship to what is around him, then issues about the origin and creation of this existence were bound to come up and needed to be answered.

These issues however were not the main cause of Arjuna's dilemma. As such these issues have been dealt in Gita fundamentally in the contextual sense, as the basis of the total philosophical design, as a backdrop. Sometimes they appear to be rather terse.

This is because any lengthy explanation on the issue was not the need of the hour.

Krishna tells Arjuna that the entire existence, whatever he can see or touch in this world is His *Maya*, His creative power. (VII-14)

I am the origin of all this world , And its' dissolution as well. (VII - 6)

For all this is my creative power, Divine, hard to transcend. (VII - 14)

Existence is not the product of God's *Maya* but *Maya* itself. *Maya* is a very commonly used term in the Indian/Hindi parlance. The word *Maya* has been variably interpreted by the scholars. Many translate it as 'illusion', that is imaginary. Some interpret it as the wonder of creation, the creative power of god. Some understand it as life, the existence, the creation itself, and whatever keeps happening in this existing cosmic system. For them it is a continuous source of energy, which keeps the wheel of *Brahma* rotating.

Is Existence An Illusion ?

There is a prominent school of thought in the Hindu philosophy, which treats life and the entire world as an illusion. Gita does not treat the world as an illusion. Life, or this universe is not just an illusion. It is real, at least for the living individual it is real. One cannot physically get out of this thing called existence. There is no other space anywhere. That is why renunciation (*Sanyas*) is not the solution to anything. Even as man (*Sanyasi*) tries to renounce and escape he remains bound to the world system of living. This is the system of *Maya*, of creation.

From the individual's point of view, however since it is god's creation, it can get uncreated also. Thus it is temporary, it is eternal for the individual. This is because man's life time itself is finite, not eternal. Thus this entire existence is an illusion only in the sense that as far as the individual is concerned it is a very temporary and transitory phenomenon. Death makes it lack permanence and stability from his perspective.

Strangely death is the only certainty of life, and that is what makes the whole creation ephemeral for the individual. For the physical being, death means the end of the whole world because how can there be anything still there for the individual when he himself is no more.

Even if one accepts the phenomenon of an immortal soul, as propounded in some of the Upanishads, even then one has to remember that the existence as we perceive, is something which has certain physical qualities. We can see, touch, smell, hear and understand by our minds the various facets of this existence. With death our capacity for such perception/understanding also dies because all these are the faculties of the sensory organs of the body which also die. The soul being pure and unaffected by such material stimuli (as soul is described in all the texts including Gita) would hence remain incapable of interacting with the external existence in the way the body does.

The soul would thus also be incapable of retaining impression of any of the impulses to which the body had been subjected to after the mortal body dies. Thus if the soul transmigrates it cannot carry forward any of the qualities of the relinquished body, and thus of the mind, because these things have not contaminated the soul. Thus for the body, and its residential faculties, death is an absolutely terminal phenomenon. For the individual it is the end of the world. The existence of a soul inside him really does not help the individual in any practical/material way.

If we examine this argument from the scientific point of view also, we have to accept that the entire existence for an individual is there only through the medium of his sensory faculties. It is only the transmission of certain messages (stimuli) through our sensory systems, and their subsequent recapitulation in our minds into something sensible, that this world exists. Whatever we sense we accept as existing. All these transmissions are done by small electric currents, i.e., passing of electrons through our nervous systems. Human nervous system is a sort of electric network, and the entire system of perception is through a chain of electrical impulses. In the brain also the activity of receiving, understanding, remembering and ordering of an action or emotion is basically an electro-chemical activity. Our thinking machinery is nothing but a center of chemical reactions.

No one really knows how the world is. It is only the brain's perception/interpretation (by means of electro-chemical reactions) of the impulses/electric signals sent by the receptor organs like eye, ear, skin, etc. in response to external stimuli. These organs actually do not see or hear anything themselves but simply receive messages of sight, sound, touch, etc. and pass on the message to the brain to make sense out of it. And hence occur the frequent known confusions and mix-ups. Reality is also thus only a recreation or recapitulation of a perception.

Other life sustaining activities of the body are also like wise. The body lives because an electric beat arising out of nowhere in the Sinu-auricular node of our hearts keep ticking without our knowledge or volition. It keeps our hearts working day in and day out. Thus the continuation of life, and the apparent existence of the entire creation is in our minds, out of a process of passage of electrons and a chain of chemical reactions. And once this current stops, there is no more anything of the creation. The whole existence vanishes for the individual in a moment like snapping of a cord. To that extent the whole creation is an illusion. It all sounds so mundane, so hygienically dry, so clinical, so un-divine, so scary.

Krishna tells Arjuna He is the being as well as the non-being, the existent as well as the non-existent. (IX-19). The same thing was said about *Brahma* in the Vedas and the Upanishads. *Maya* is this quality of evolution of the system of reality from the system of non-reality. It is the power, which makes the existence transient within the permanent. *Maya* is the wonder of this cycle of interchangeability between the living and the non-living, between the being and the non-being. The existence has always been there, it shall always be there, because *Brahma* (matter) is indestructible/imperishable yet for the individual it is transitory and temporary. This feature of reality within the lack of reality is one aspect of *Maya*.

Maya is thus neither just an illusion nor just the material existence but the entire cosmic design in the most holistic sense of the term.

Brahma, the Creator

Krishna further says that He is The Time. (XI-32)

The only two eternal, infinite and imperishable things in the entire existence are time and space. There was never, and can never be, a time when time was not existing. What Stephen Hawking says about Time is relative Time and not absolute Time.

Similarly there can be no place where space is absent. Everywhere is time and space. It has always been so. There is no other way. Whatever end we try to conceive about existence, we have to think of what is beyond the end. Nowhere can time and space terminate in absolute terms. There would still be space and time left.

Time cannot have any origin or end. It has no age. Similarly existence has to be infinite and indestructible. These two, time and space, are and can be, the only fundamental dimensions in existence or imagination. (The three dimensions that we commonly speak of are actually only the co-ordinates of the dimension of Space.) Nothing can be conceived out of these two dimensions. And these two co-exist in harmony, always and everywhere. And hence there can be no question of anyone creating the existence from outside because the two eternal dimensions cannot have a Zero - point. That is why *Brahma* is time and space. And Krishna, in the role of the incarnation of God Vishnu says, so about Himself.

No one knows from whence I came,
For I am the beginning of the gods themselves. (X-2)

And yet man has the limitations of time and space! He is bound by himself. He can neither extend his space nor time. That is his bond. And that is why it is imperative that the individual integrates himself with the *Brahma,* with the cosmic system. Only thus can he find liberation from all such bondage!

What term do we give to this phenomenon, to this system of bondage and liberation ? And how do we term this cosmic order ? Divine creation ?

To the traditionally religious minded the answer may be an emphatic 'yes'. But in Gita, or for that matter in the entire Indian philosophy anything as 'divine creation' has to be very different, very qualified, very subtle. The subject of creation has been discussed sporadically and intermittently in different chapters of Gita. Co-relating them, we find that Gita holds the view that the world was created, and is being operated by a supreme, eternal but unaffected power and it is impossible to fathom or fully comprehend it.

The Creator, the God of Gita is of a different class. He is without emotions and does not take mundane (earthly) day-to-day decisions on living beings. But the system runs with/because of His power/energy. That is His *Maya.* (IX-9)

And that is why the Upanishads give emphasis to understanding of *Brahma,* to integration of self with *Brahma,* rather than to the worship of *Brahma.*

We are still left with the question as to why was it created ? Why is it run in this particular way ? What is the underlying principle ? And what is the purpose behind the whole endeavour and enterprise, if any ?

The System

Krishna says that the world system is so because it is His resolve, His desire, that is all. In fact these things are not to be revealed to anyone. They are mysterious. These questions can be sensed and understood only at the metaphysical level.

At the physical level Gita remains esoteric on these questions because giving such explanations was not the objective of the discourse. The objective was to make the individual, Arjuna, realise his position and his entity in this system which he neither has created nor has any control over.

One may accept what we may call the Indian philosophy/theory of creation. One may have faith in the *Genesis* of the Old Testament, which tells us of God creating the world in six days. Or one may believe only the scientific theories like the Big Bang theory of cosmic creation, Hubbell's proposition of expanding universe, the Darwinian theory of evolution. Whatever one may believe in the fact remains that we have no control over the cosmic design/system. Whatever theory, philosophy or religion one may have belief in, it does not alter this material fact.

What we sometimes feel, as science having taken charge of the system, is a very superficial view. Science has been able to just tinker with the system a bit at the best. Even that is at the question of 'how'. As regards the question of 'why at all,' there is no scientific answer. There cannot be one. There cannot be a logical explanation for everything. Why water freezes at zero degrees or why the structure of atom is in the way it is ? Why is life ? And why is death ? There are no logical answers to such things. This is the system. This is the *Maya*.

The Individual

Krishna advises Arjuna that he should know, and accept this *Maya* as it is, and try to realise his own identity, his own real self, in this context of inevitability of what he has, where he is. He should also be able to see what is beyond the superficial facade of sensory perception, what is unveiled, what is absolute (not in relation to self). He should know what is apparent and what is not and be able to distinguish between the two. Arjuna should accept the eternity of the existence, the irreversibility of the system, the infinite expanse of time and space, the limitation of the lifetime, the constraints of his choices and scope of action, the reality of his situation. This realisation and acceptance alone would bring him peace and equanimity of mind.

It is not that some god would bestow anything upon the individual outside of the world system through divine intervention. One can get nothing out of an imaginary God. But by devotion, by understanding, by changing one's outlook, by *Yoga*, by developing the capacity to perceive through the veils of what is apparent, *Maya*, one can free oneself from the confusions, delusions and hence from their bondage in this life. (VII-17)

Is There Aany Purpose of Life ?

Then what is the purpose behind the whole thing? Is there any ? How do we know for certainty?

There are certain philosophies, which hold that man was created to serve or to glorify God. Some propagate that man is born to serve other human beings. These altruistic thoughts mostly belong to the religious category.

The Existentialist philosophy does not believe that there is any intrinsic purpose of life and propounds that we are here just like that. It also suggests that since we are to be here we may as well assume a purpose to give a reason to our existence (*raison de etre*), that since we do not have any objective value or reason to live we must assume reasons, i.e., we must rationalise what is.

Gita does not reveal any divine purpose of life as such. Any such declaration would have been beyond the realm of rational thought and scientific/objective explanation. Perhaps it was also not germane to the issue. The fact is that there is a universe, and we have a life, this is how it is, take it or leave it. The relevant question is that since we have a life how do we live through it. We have to live, because it is our most fundamental nature, and our instinct to survive goads us to continue. And for this perpetuation we have to act. What else can one do with/in life ? Action is a necessity, it is unavoidable. But in the process of action we meet with problems, dilemmas and contradictions which confuse us. At crossroads our survival instinct is threatened thereby causing loss of peace of mind. This leads to pain and suffering and sadness.

We all need peace because it gives us a sense of security, a positive stroke to our survival instinct. It is not only in our own interest but rather the need of our true nature to be at peace with ourselves. That is why peace of mind is desirable and rated so high.

So how does one go about the process where one has to act and still be at peace?

The basic flaw of the theories involving divinity is that they are not entirely convincing to the scientific/rational mind. Altruism though sounds good seems to be not entirely in conformity with basic human nature. The process of struggle for survival was a very ruthless one and so has it made the instinctive human nature, a very ruthless one. The drawback of the atheistic/existentialist thinking is that it makes life a very morose and morbid affair. One may keep looking out for a reason to exist and may not find one anywhere.

Both religions and philosophies are also often about what is right and what is wrong, what is good and what is bad. Gita does not indulge in any such sermonising. No code of personal or social life is stipulated in Gita. In fact in Chapter V (verses 14-15) Krishna states that god neither creates the situations for actions, good or bad, nor does god regard actions as good (pious) or sins. The god of Gita is above such mundane and petty things. In fact since the god, as *Brahma,* resides in the individual himself, it is for the individual to derive happiness by working for the general good.

Krishna is, in the worldly sense, Arjuna's friend as well as his spiritual guide as much as He is the mythological incarnation of Lord Vishnu. Krishna speaks at two levels, the earthly and the metaphysical. Thus we find two sets of values relative and absolute. Arjuna is at liberty to take the message of Krishna (Gita) at his own level. At the mundane level Arjuna should understand the compulsions of his body and its faculties, intellect and nature, and at the same time he should try to reconcile with the world system, the *Maya*. Only such reconciliation would bring peace.

It is only for the purpose of making Arjuna understand the world system or *Maya* that Krishna explains the concept of nature of the qualities of nature, about how nature interacts with the body and forces decision making. Thus understanding of the working of the world system in totality is of fundamental importance for understanding the philosophy of Gita.

6

ACTION AND DETACHMENT

Gita begins with the question of Arjuna as to how should he act in the given situation. Whether to act at all or not ? Action and detachment are the two most important issues of the entire Bhagavad Gita. In order to understand the theory of detachment it would be necessary for us to firstly examine what is action.

We all act, all the time. Why do we act ?

Action is a must to sustain life. It is a sort of instinctive compulsion for survival. In the first stages the actions are for physical survival and once that is assured the actions are for psychological survival, which is basically an extension of the physical instinct for survival. These are two related and overlapping levels of human existence. The management theorist Maslow has given it the term of 'Hierarchy of needs'.

Life of abdication or self denial is truly speaking a self deception. It is contrary to our nature which wants us to survive, to perpetuate and to fulfill. *Sanyas* (renunciation) adopted physically, without being in the state of detachment, physically as well as mentally, is sheer escapism. It can only make life without a reason. Curbing one's nature is not conducive to inner harmony also. As the individual tries to constrain himself to an acquired lifestyle it leads to an inner conflict. Hence it cannot give peace of mind. Such a life of surrender can only exude a facade of tranquillity. At best whatever real peace so obtained would be superficial and ephemeral. It is also not practically possible for most of the individuals to live so.

As action is unavoidable we may think why we act in the way we do ?

Compulsions of Nature

Actions are classified as voluntary and involuntary. Each organ of our body, each cell, acts for the purpose of survival, voluntarily and involuntarily, knowingly and unknowingly. This distinction is purely in the physical (medical) sense. Involuntary actions are also called reflex actions in as much as they do not involve application of mind but are spontaneous reactions of the body as a part of its intrinsic survival mechanism. But voluntary actions mean actions done out of consideration and thought. It also entails availability of options, and choice, that is why they are out of volition.

But to what extend do we really have the choice ? The sense of responsibility, and hence of guilt arises out of this feeling (impression) of availability of options and exercise of volition. In other terms we can also say that whereas reflex actions are necessitated by the body the so called voluntary actions are necessitated by the total system of which the individual is also a part.

Actions are thus intrinsically related to the way man looks at himself and at his environment, the world. They involve man's perception of the physical existence in which he is situated. In a way they are the reflection of one's intrinsic perception of life. But why does an individual perceive a situation in a particular way ? What guides his psyche, and hence his behaviour ? It is again his survival instinct, which guides him towards a certain course of action. That is what becomes his intrinsic nature. It may vary from person to person. One may feel that fighting it out is the best way to survive while another may feel that running away is a better option, and yet another person may that feel submission/surrender is the best option. It may also be a combination of such options. That is what makes the human psychology (nature) so complicated and idiosyncratic. These are the traits/ tendencies or constituents of nature which are discussed at length in Gita.

And man is compelled to act by his nature. One knows he is like to commit himself to a certain course of action and does so in spite of himself. Evil tendencies compel the individual to do evil against his wishes and cool reasoning. (III-36). And that is why some people try such restrain on themselves, as they are doubtful how they will react to a particular situation on the spur of the moment. People even wonder why they reacted in the way they did. That is because of the permanent constituents of their innate nature. There are also momentary/transitory constituents, called phases of moods which also affect the way we react. For the same situation we may behave differently at different times. They all constitute our nature. And so one's intrinsic nature is one of the most compelling factors affecting one's actions.

Many of us suffer from psychological complexes of insecurity, inferiority, envy, etc. We keep brooding- Why are we not like that, why our lot is not better than others ? Even for most trifle things we suffer such pains, tensions and anxieties, almost helplessly because of our internal way of perception.

Then there are externally imposed factors as well.

Compulsions of Situation

In the course of a war, is it not surprising that one human being shoots another who is a perfect stranger to him and has done him no personal harm? It is even more surprising that he voluntarily and proudly stretches his own neck out to be slit by another stranger to whom he has done no harm. Both actions appear to be very irrational. Yet man does so, just because he has to carry a flag. Maybe it is a cause to him. He fights for an idea. At least he thinks so. But is it not that what we call our convictions, our beliefs, are actually beliefs which were successfully planted from outside for some other reason, and the idea survived, nay thrived ? But what made the individual accept the idea to the core of his mind that he is ready to get himself killed for it ?

Or maybe he was compelled by the circumstances. What choice did the individual have in the above given situation ?

We think that what we do is our own voluntary action. But can there be any action, which can be called purely an individua's own action ? We act in a particular way either because we are by nature like that, or because our situation has caused it to be so. Or perhaps we act out of a synthesis of the two factors. In a way, there is no such thing as an absolute individual action. There are only reactions. What we think is our action/decision is actually only a reaction of our psyche to some other (re)action in the time (environment) and space frame.

Could we have done otherwise ? Is it possible for the individual to avoid or deviate from the course of action he takes in the given situation with his existent nature ? To what extent ? If he could have then why that did not get done ? Why the fanatic decides on a suicide mission rather than live a life of peace and pleasure ? He must have compulsions, both external and internal. This is the interplay or the dynamics of the mind and the matter, creating situations for action.

This is not to say that the individual's action has no meaning or that he has no choice. The individual will is there and man has a choice over his actions but its role is limited in the sense that nothing can be working in isolation. There is no original or absolute action. The individual action is a part in the chain of a mammoth, complex and extremely dynamic system, and the individual has no control over rest of the system. And his own actions are also but in a way only resonating expressions of reactions to the dynamics of the system. That is to say that actions are taking place out of an interplay/dialectics between the human nature and his situation. And man is just the instrument for the implementation of the process.

What then is the relationship between our actions and their outcome ? Can there be any ? And is it possible for the doer to have any control over the outcome/result of the deed under such compelling circumstances ? Are occurrences just the result of situations where human will and endeavour has little significance ?

Hegel, the great idealist philosopher of Germany, in a different context, commented upon how things take shape. He used the term 'dialectic' to describe how the World Spirit unfolds itself. He was of the view that in the context of interaction between mind and the matter the mind (universal thought) has the upper hand. Karl Marx turned Hegel's dialectics upside down and asserted the significance of matter shaping the mind.

In fact life experiences show that there is no finality of this dialectics and this interplay is a continuous process of life. Occurrence of things in existence is an outcome of this process of dialectics and continuous dis-equilibrium. Gita holds this view of continuous flux.

A brief look into the history of recent times shows how this cycle works. There are repeated manifestations of destinies being shaped out of situations. After the World War I, Hitler emerged out of the German sense of anger and humiliation of the Treaty of Versailles. He was nurtured by the bourgeoisie due to their own fear of growing communism in Europe. Without that particular set of circumstances Hitler may not have developed the nature he did, and even with the same mental makeup, would not have succeeded in capturing power in Germany. Hitler was as much a victim of his circumstances as the millions who got killed 'because of him'.

Lenin could not have contributed lesser for the Bolshevik revolution in Russia. He was in exile in Europe, in obscurity and despair. But the World War I and the Czar Nicholas II did everything that was needed. In the situation of the political and social flux that emerged after the soldiers' mutiny in Russia, Lenin merely filled the vacant slot at the right time. Even Napoleon Bonaparte did the same in the aftermath of the French revolution to capture power in France. But what could he do at St. Helena? He did not change but the situation had changed. No action was possible or worthwhile there at St. Helena, except to be lost in oblivion.

Back home in India, a hundred years earlier Mahatma Gandhi would have been premature and would have gone unnoticed. In his time he was able to shake the British empire. Today new social gods have been dug out of their black holes and the relevance of Mahatma Gandhi is openly being questioned.

The rise of many other great heroes of our times similarly are stories of circumstances opening out situations for meteoritic rise of their heroes, throwing them up when they are needed and then throwing them out when they become redundant for the situation. Churchill's rise and fall in his political life is another one of such tales.

They might also be called as men of destiny. But one cannot have destiny in isolation. Destiny cannot be absolute. It has to be relative, contextual, situational, dynamic and transitory. Had there not been men like Hitler, Lenin, Napoleon or Gandhi in the times when they came up history might have taken a different course. But these same men in different times and different contexts would have been redundant and unknown. They on their own steam could not have created the history they did.

Thus individual achievements are actually only fulfillment's of the gaps created in the system by the system for the system. The individual merely fills the slot, like tools. They are thus instruments to fulfillment of a destiny of the system, which is unknown and continuously unfolding itself out of its own contradictions and internal dynamics.

Dynamics of the System

A person who qualifies for a job, gets a promotion, wins an election or a race is only filling the void, the slots, which the system has created (got created inside the system, because of the system). Bridging these gaps is the requirement of the system. Each slot filled leads to new openings, creating further opportunities for actions. And so the process goes on and on in a very dynamic and fluid state. This is also to illustrate why some people succeed while others do not. When we read of success stories we read about the intelligence the effort and the perseverance of the individual who has succeeded. At the time we accept these as the final factors of success we should also remember that we are mocking at hundreds of other individuals who had more intelligence and had put in more hard work but did not succeed. Their efforts get belittled only because they did not succeed. That is what we call as nothing succeeding like success. Why did they not succeed? Did the system have no slot for them? Maybe! Krishna does accept that providence is one of the five factors causing an action.

Further, the individual's actions in this state of flux are not just his own voluntary (predetermined) actions but are reactions within the system. He has a choice but the choice is also created by the system over which he has no control. The choice is further conditioned by the individuals own physical and mental nature. In other words, individual actions are an outcome of the dynamics of the system. The individual's will/choice/option/is still there but its role is limited as the individual has no control over what is other than him. And further, the whole thing is transitory and ephemeral.

An individual's action is actually thus nothing but a very small ripple in the ocean of the entire cosmic design. As such it can have only equally little bearing on the outcome. The individual has little or no control over the results. And since his own actions also are conditioned/forced/caused/manipulated by a multitude of extraneous factors over which he has no control, he has in effect little control over his own actions as well. Even as he carries the impression that all the decisions/actions taken by him are of his own making, he actually is just the medium through which the act is being conducted. Thus he alone is neither responsible for his actions nor has he any control over its consequences. The two are not and cannot be considered as directly linked.

This sounds disturbing. Gita explains how we can come to terms with something we are neither responsible for nor have control over. This is possible by realising our nature and our entity in the overall cosmic design. Then where is the room for the sense of achievement, responsibility or failure on the part of the single individual ? What then is the rationale to have ego or attachment ? Then where is the room for dilemma ? Why then the remorse or the despair ? The concept of detachment emanates out of this logic.

When Krishna says that the mystery of the cosmic design cannot be understood by anyone, He is in fact only stressing that man has little options and no control over the grand cosmic design. As such it is better to accept this phenomenon, try to understand ourselves and develop attitudes to come to terms with the realities of life, to try to merge our nature in synthesis and harmony with the mysterious and the unknowable, and uncontrollable.

This is a state of mind, a system of thinking process. It can be achieved by, and would at the same time lead to, detachment. A person so composed, who has been able to integrate his existence with what is around him, his nature with the cosmic system, in a harmonious synthesis, through rational and logical thinking, is called a *Yogi*.

Detachment

Earlier in this book it has been stressed that human action is guided by self preservation instincts. One acts to achieve something. It would be, and is, thus natural to be attached to ones' actions and desire favourable outcome of the actions towards the goals at which the actions have been directed at. We all find people acting vigorously in areas which interest them, in which they have a stake and hence attachment or commitment. The fields with which people are not attached are ignored, and no action is taken by the individuals in the areas that do not concern or interest them. Thus to propose action without attachment would appear to be psychologically discordant, contrary, incongruous and anomalous.

Is then the concept of detachment not against human nature ? Action with detachment appears to be inversely related ideas.

Is there then any logical contradiction or inconsistency within the philosophy of Gita? Why otherwise would one act at all ?

No ! Gita does not stand for inaction. In fact it strongly advocates action. That is what Krishna keeps telling Arjuna, to act. He repudiates renunciation. Then what is the concept of detachment ?

Detachment is neither purposelessness nor is not disinterest. It is not indifference either. It is neither abdication nor abstinence nor is it self denial. It is neither renunciation of the physical act, i.e., *sanyas*, nor is it a life of prayer and devotion alone. Gita is not concerned about the outward appearances at all. The exteriors and the cosmetics of lifestyle do not matter.

The detached person is not one who does not desire achievements. After all Arjuna is exhorted to enter the battlefield for the sake of the kingdom, for personal glory, for righteousness, and for fulfillment of his nature as a warrior. In fact making efforts for excellence is one of the fundamental teachings of Gita. The detached person does not abjure achievements. Such an attitude is neither expected nor advocated. Detachment is not lack of desire for the fruits of one's actions nor lack of desire for action itself. It is simply the awareness and acceptance of the fact that actions and results both are not directly linked, because of the limited role of the individual's action. And thus the *yogi* is unaffected by the results. Thus he is unattached to the affect of the results of his actions.

Detachment is all about how we look at things. The detached individual does work for achievement. He is different from others only in the sense that he is aloof, he does not feel himself personally involved with his actions, he does not link his actions with the possibility of their achievements.

In the much quoted verse 47 of Chap. II, Krishna uses the term - '*do not become the cause of results*'. (Too often this verse is seen wrongly translated as- 'Action is thy duty, fruits are not thy concern.') This is to say that one should not consider himself as the instrument which will produce results. One can only act. That is what is in one's control, perhaps. So one can consider himself as the doer (responsible for) only to the extent of the execution of the act. The results, being out of one's control, the individual should not think himself as the cause for the fruition of results.

Hence achievements or failures of his actions do not affect the *yogi*. He is only concerned about the actions his work requires. He acts because he has a purpose, which he must pursue, as if he is compelled to act for it, as a duty, to keep the world system going, knowingly. He acts for the purpose, but then he is linked to the area of action alone and is not linking himself to the outcome. He is happy to work for the sake of work itself, as a duty he has to do.

Detachment is basically de-linking of what we do from what we receive back from the system. This de-linking is out of a conscious decision, arrived at rationally, by the individual himself. It becomes the operating system of the thinking of the *yogi*. It is a rational decision of a person who has understood his place in the universal setup. Once the individual realises and accepts who he is, where he stands and what is his significance, his outlook changes. He views the things in a different perspective altogether. There is no room for disillusionment as there is no illusion, and hence no loss of peace of mind. He would thus find a total transformation of his personality.

Introspection

It is necessary to understand one's own nature in order to be really detached. One should have the courage to accept firstly that 'I am like that.' Once the individual understands his true nature he can then place himself in the context of the world system and identify his problems. He can question himself as to why does he feel so involved that he suffers the pains of failure, envy and anxiety. How important and permanent are these causes ? Why are the issues so dear to him ?

Such questioning will induce discernment. Then he should ask as to what should be done in a particular situation, and what can he do. Once the course of action has been rationally thought of he should pursue that and not be worried about the consequences, thinking that he has done whatever he could have done and that getting worried would not help either way. That would be the practical application of the principle of detachment.

And so teaches Krishna that Arjuna should fight in the battle because it is a justified cause, because it is his duty to fight for his righteous cause and he should not think of the consequences of the act which he is duty bound to do. Such an action is a detached action.

7

YOGI : THE NON-DOER

Work, and hence life becomes a bondage only because of our attachment to the results of our actions, our expectations/apprehensions. Since outcome depends on things unknown, uncontrolled, para-rational, it is illogical to have attachment.

By the same logic, we also derive to the conclusion that since the dynamics of the entire cosmic design can neither be understood nor controlled by the individual, it would be rational not to link one's actions to the results. And so one should have neither the attachment to one's action nor should one have the ego of being the doer. Such feelings are in fact illusions and lead to mental disquiet.

The principle of detachment may sound difficult to practice. How does the *Yogi* think as he acts, so as to feel detached ? Gita provides a pragmatic approach to the situation, i.e., *nishkama karma* (detached action).

Nishkama Karma

The knowledgeable individual, the *yogi*, continues with his duties, actions and worldly chores in accordance to his nature and worldly requirements, while being fully conscious of his position, his significance, and lack of it. He realises his being, his existence not in isolation but in the context of the entire cosmic design and the demands/compulsions of the design.

He knows he is a creature of his nature, his situation and his consciousness and his actions are involuntarily taking place out of their interactions. He feels as if the system is operating on its own and his physical being, as a part of the system, is being used by the system as an instrument of expression of that system, in spite of and away from his self. He feels that whatever is happening is a manifestation of an unknowable and uncontrollable design, and he is being made to act/work by the system. As he realises himself in the grand design, the *Yogi* feels that even as he works he is not doing anything. Work is taking place on its own. Only his body and its faculties, i.e., the mind and the sensory organs are working, that too under the compulsion/influence of nature while he himself is not doing anything at all. His work thus becomes *nishkama karma*.

Detachment is only the first phase towards attainment of the stage of being a *Yogi*, the accomplished one. Realisation of this non-acted action completes his integration with the mystic system, the *Maya*. He cannot have attachment to something he has not done, he being a non-doer, and *Maya* getting the acts done. The cycle of the self logic is thus completed and runs both ways. Since he is not doing anything there is no reason for attachment, and he is not the doer because he is unattached. *Nishkama-karma* can also thus be called as detached action.

The *yogi* is performing all his duties. There is no dereliction in his works. Only difference is that he views himself as an outsider now, while the body is conducting the functions under the co-ordination of the mind. It is someone else doing the works. He himself is out of it.

He feels he is a player enacting a given role (assignment) in the drama of *maya*. He has no personal stake in it because there is nothing personal in this existence. Everything belongs to *Brahma*. It is only this draining out of personal involvement from the cycle of actions being done by the physical being which distinguishes action from *nishkama karma*.

Sambhava – Even Mindedness

Sambhava means sameness of attitude, to all people and to all situations. It was the precursor to the modern day concept of secularism. The beauty lies in the metaphysical logic behind the need to adopt sameness of attitude.

Gita does not expect uniformity or equality. It is impossible for everyone to be same or equal. Variation is inherent in nature. What is required however is that one should accept these variations as facets and parts of the grand cosmic design which emanates out of a single source, *Brahma*. Fundamentally everything being *Brahma*, is same. And hence one should adopt a sameness of attitude towards the externally apparent facets, realising that this variation of living beings and of situations is essentially superficial, and behind all this is the1 same *Brahma*.

Hence realising, one should treat everything and everyone equally without getting affected or deluded by this variation. Shri Krishna says that the *Yogi* sees the same *Brahma* in the Brahmin, in the pariah, in the cow and in the dog. (V-18)

One who is able to perceive himself and his situation so objectively and feels detached, one who reaches this mental stage is freed from the bondage of works because then the results do not affect him. If he succeeds, he does not feel exhilarated because he feels he has not done anything. He takes success without pride or euphoria. If he fails he does not feel the pain or guilt of failure.

He remains calm and steady in all situations, unaffected. This state is described as *sambhava* or sameness of feeling/attitude. He thus attains supreme bliss, contentment within oneself, and peace of mind.

One who has achieved such a state of detachment does not have to change his actions or alter his material life style at all. Since his outlook has changed by such self realisation, all that happens is that he is no more swayed by the trifles of the material world. He is aware of his role in the overall design. He knows himself and hence is neither deluded nor disillusioned by transitory fruits of life or by lack of them. He does not gain control over anything material nor can he change anything. He simply gains control over himself by this change of his own outlook. He feels liberated from the impulses of his attachments. Now he can change the way he looks at his world!

In his actions the *Yogi* is unbiased because he is not attached. In fact he is not attached even to his own decisions (VI-9). He does not feel that he has taken the decision. He is just the medium for the making of the decision, which the system is taking through him. Hence there is no room for regret, failure or disillusionment for him. And since there are no more concepts of gains or losses for him, there is no more any room for pain, pleasure, misery or remorse.

For the rational mind there is also no room for ego because the *Yogi* knows that he is not doing or achieving anything.

He does in fact not even feel guilty of any wrong he has done. It is the system, which is working in that direction, in spite of himself. This however should not be construed as or confused with freedom to act as one wishes. It is not to inculcate irresponsibility. Gita does not give license to act without wisdom and sense of righteousness. The *yogi* is detached from the results but as far as the act itself is concerned the *yogi* does what is righteous and dutiful to him. He has to apply his mind and act for what is good for all.

This sense of consciously endeavouring to excel in good work is what distinguishes *sambhava* from fatalism. Fatalism is something negative, where you leave things to the fate in a resigned sort of way. Gita does not advocate fatalism. It urges man to act, and act in a positive way, and for the right cause. Because, irrespective of the result, it is the sense of endeavour for the right cause which is more likely to give peace and satisfaction than mere achievement. And the cause for action should be for good of the people. Since practicing evil consciously cannot bring peace to anyone he must work for general good and find happiness in doing it well.

The *Yogi* acts fully aware of all this and finds bliss in action which is now a way of practicing detachment for him. He finds fulfillment of his own self in action. And so he realises his full potential in actions. Since he is unaffected either by the act or by its consequence, there is nothing that can stop him from his mission, which he has derived from his natural self. Even while fully amidst action he is at peace with himself, and what is around him, because he has elevated himself from everything that is other than his self. His mental equilibrium is never disturbed, because he knows that any type of inclination in thought or action causes a reaction resulting in disturbance of the equilibrium. Thus he attains liberation/salvation from work even as he is working.

He accepts his position, nature, duties, work and actions as a part of the cosmic design unraveling itself out of its own compulsion, an act over which he is not to get involved as he can neither control it nor is responsible for it. He has no reason to get attached, either to the system or to his own actions.

Karma Yoga

The way this cosmic system works can neither be understood nor can be it controlled by anyone, says Gita. Even Krishna cannot predict or alter the course of events that are set to take place. If He could, He may have averted the bloodshed of the battle, or at least predicted what would happen. Destiny has to pursue its own course of action, and everyone has to do his own lot. Whether we accept Krishna's verdict about divine creation and His omnipotence or not, we have to accept that we have no control over the cosmic system. Where does the individual stand in this scenario?

He still retains control over his thoughts. Maybe he cannot change what is but he can always change his outlook, see things differently, give reasons of his own where no reason is apparent. What else is the choice anyway? One has to continue with the life cycle and its chores. The option is how we decide to take it. Reality is thus not just what is. It becomes what we decide. Hence the *yogi* creates his own world and seeks contentment in it, in the sense that he seeks his inner self, that subtle essence of *Brahma* in himself, integrates with it, and finds liberation. And hence he becomes *Brahma*, his own god.

And Krishna says that He pervades among all of us but we are unable to discern this. That is how God is omnipresent.

One might again question that if everything is temporary, transitory and beyond control of the individual, why should anyone work at all ?

Work is essential not only for sustaining life but also because it is the pursuit of excellence in work that alone can give real happiness. If mind is not leashed towards working for righteousness it will be led astray by the senses which crave for results. This will lead to tensions and conflicts. There is no real happiness in such a situation of anxiety. Peace of mind is the foundation of happiness. Detachment provides the peace and work provides the space and scope for happiness in a creativity, which is unburdened with results. Such a work is self-satisfying and self-sustaining. While working so, the individual needs no external stimuli (rewards or commendation) for happiness. That is the real liberation of the individual, a liberation from the physical and virtual external forces of bondage. It is a liberation from the bondage of works through the work itself. There is no liberation from or without work.

Knowing oneself, one's own true nature is essential for such liberation. Not knowing ourselves is often a basic cause of our problems. We want something but our nature may not be suitable for the path to its achievement. Even the destination may not be what we imagine it to be. Yet we suffer from the complexes and make ourselves unhappy. In extreme cases such uncontrolled thinking may lead to schizophrenia or split personality in the individual.

In the Upanishads it is often mentioned that one should question himself 'Who I am?' One should meditate on it so that one is clear in his mind about himself. Only then, when false notions about oneself are removed, can one perceive the external issues with detached discernment and take rational decisions.

This is one way of synthesising/integrating oneself (creating harmony) with the *Brahma,* to attain the supreme state of *Brahma.*

The all pervading nature, the *Brahma,* and the man's inner self are the two eternally pure things for they both have their source of origin in the imperishable : Peace is to be obtained through realisation of their unision. One cannot be happy by trying to be what one is really not. An individual in such a situation would feel as if he is walking around the world with a mask. A hypocrite can never be happy, a crook may be, at least temporarily. So one has to be true to his self for achieving peace of mind. This has to be done by cool and ruthless reasoning.

The concept of *nishkama karma* or detached action or simply detachment has to be arrived at through such rational decision making. By consistent and conscious efforts one should dispel one's own confusions/illusions. One should be able to identify what is one best suited for, and accept it (be content with it). It would be an exercise of moulding the way of one's thought process. One has to train one's mind to achieve this outlook. It must become a permanent state of mind and should always reflect in action. If one's nature is to act or one is compelled to act one should carry out the works as *nishkama karma.* Such a pursuit of action is *Karma Yoga,* that is integration (with self/*Brahma*) through action.

One should be able to see oneself from a distance, away from self, and watch how the mind in co-ordination with the sensory faculties of the body, and with the body, conducts itself in the pursuit of life and survival in the world environment. The forces of nature pull the mind in different directions, to pursue particular courses of actions. One who can see himself so objectively has done true introspection and can pursue action without detachment.

In Chapter XII, Krishna explains that there are many ways in which a person can find salvation depending on his nature and capabilities. Though integration with the *Brahma* is the most sublime way, it is difficult for a lay person to understand, accept and integrate himself with the concept of an abstract and formless *Brahma* and so Gita advocates devotion through a form (idol) as also acceptable. In fact, meditation, faithful devotion, performance of rightful actions done without attachment, and works done for general good are all various ways for attainment of the same supreme state of perfection.

The *Sankhya* philosophy, advocated by sage Kapila, stresses on wisdom and renunciation of works while the *karma yoga* stresses achievement of perfection through performance of detached actions.

Pursuit of Excellence

Whereas work provides the space for peace pursuit of excellence gives dimension for a lasting happiness.

We all work. We have to. Works produce results or lead to consequences. The *yogi* is detached to the results of his works. He considers them beyond the scope of his consideration because he feels he is not the doer and has no control over the consequences. However the action part of the work is under the control of the individual. It is an area available to us for seeking fulfillment by working. The *yogi* can derive satisfaction by doing his work to the best of his ability. What you cannot control you should not rely upon for peace and happiness. If you depend on something you do not/cannot control then you become a slave of that outside factor. Gita seeks to liberate us from the bondage of our works. If we think only of what we have to do, and do it well, then we act like masters of the situation. As such the *yogi* de-links himself from the results which his actions may contribute to cause, and concentrates only on the actions.

A *karma yogi* is thus a person who performs all his duties, keeping only righteousness in mind and being detached to the fruits of his actions.

It is recognised the world over that there is nothing like self-motivation actuated by the desire for self-satisfaction in the pursuit of excellence. Pursuit of excellence is better than pursuit of ambition because ambition involves attachment and hence entails unhappiness if the ambition is not achieved. However there is no such barrier in the pursuit of excellence. If we have to do a thing we may as well do it well and feel happy about it. As such the discerning individual will seek satisfaction and self-contentment in the pursuit of excellence in his works without being distracted by the affects of the results.

Krishna advises Arjuna to become a *karma yogi*, a person who finds peace through work. There are many ways to find peace and happiness. One may find peace by knowledge of *Brahma*, by identifying himself with *Brahma*. It may not be the way for others. It depends on the nature of the individual. For a warrior like Arjuna peace, fulfillment and happiness, and thus mental salvation/liberation from what he is doing, lies in action, in pursuit of an action which is without selfish motives, without personal desires and personal attachments. As such Arjuna must pursue the path of *karma-yoga* for peace and happiness.

8

KARMA

These days we hear this word *karma* more than ever before. It has become fashionable to use it in a wide variety of contexts. We even hear of the Law of *karma*. What is *karma* ? What is the law of *karma* ?

The word *karma* has been variously translated and interpreted. *Karma* means work, deed or action. It also means/entails the fruit of the actions. It also entails the compulsion of the situation forcing an action to occur, forcing a person to take a particular course of action. It is thus also a part of the destiny of the doer as well as a part of his nature. *Karma* in fact includes all the four things – action, result, destiny and nature at the same time. That is so because all the four are closely related. We act according to our nature and all actions lead to reactions (results) and this cycle is destiny. The entire cycle is closely related. Let us go back to Arjuna's dilemma to examine how *karma* works.

Arjuna's dilemma whether he should participate or not in the internecine warfare for the kingdom of Hastinapur is not a superficial problem. Deep down this dilemma are very fundamental concepts that appear to be at stake, which question the entire psyche of the great archer that Arjuna is. These questions arise out of certain belief's, certain assumptions and certain values which Arjuna has held dear, which are a part of his thinking system. These values and assumptions are not intrinsically of his own. At least, not necessarily all of them. They are fundamentally a product of his environment, of the culture of his times, of his upbringing and of his life's experiences. These values are thus a creation of his perception of his experiences.

Since Arjuna's dilemma is an outcome of the way he perceives his situation we can also say that his dilemma is not absolute, and can be viewed only in relation, and in the context of his total circumstances. He is in a dilemma because he has his own sense of right and wrong. He values relationships with his loved ones, as also his right to the Pandava's claim to the kingdom of Hastinapur. He is not intrinsically against killing. After all he was a warrior, a *kshatriya,* and had slain may opponents in warfare before arriving at the battle ground of Kurukshetra. Why then is this despondency at such a crucial hour ?

Had it not been his own cousins , his dear teacher Dronacharya and his much affectionate grandfather Bhishma as his opponents, maybe he would not have had any qualms in starting the battle. Then the question of guilt, that he was to indulge in all this bloodshed for the sake of a kingdom, would not have arisen at all. So it is not the act in itself, which is causing the problem, the despondency and the dilemma. Nor is it the objective behind the act. After all Arjuna had gone out in battles and won many kingdoms before also. It is just this particular situation of killing his loved ones for the kingdom that is causing the problem.

So it is neither the act nor the objective which is causing the emotional trauma to Arjuna. It is just his perception of the act and the objectives behind the act in the particular situation, which is unacceptable to Arjuna.

The Kauravas on the other side are also battling against their kinsmen but they have no such problem of contrition. That is because they perceive the situation differently. And the Kauravas have driven the situation to the brink of the battle from which it is impossible for the Pandavas to back out. And Arjuna is compelled to fight for the cause of his brothers. This is a peculiar set of circumstances which is not of one person's making and all have to get into the act now. They seem to be thus destined for this doom of the battle. What they have to necessarily do and in consequence inevitably suffer, or gain, is their *karma*. Does the concept of *karma* then mean a predetermined destiny ?

Is there a Destiny ?

Fate and destiny have been very debatable issues of Hinduism and culture, and in fact a very strong current of fatalism in the Indian ethos is only because of a misinterpretation of the concept of *karma*. We often hear people saying that what is to happen would happen and it is the god who decides what will happen. In fact the cynical fatalists believe that god has already decided what is to be done on all issues of men and material. They believe in a predetermined fate. As an extension of this thinking, they even say that fate is determined as a judgment on the actions of the previous life. Some believe that fate is the god's reply on the works of this life itself.

Gita does not propound any theory of God meeting out judgments upon human actions. Nor is there any no concept in Gita of divine awards and punishments, during or after a person's life. (V-15) There is no concept of a Day of Judgment in Hindu philosophy. The God in Gita is without emotions or preferences. He is detached, ruthless and unaffected. And man is not a mere pawn or puppet in the hands of some divine power. Man retains his options of thought and action, of course within the limitations discussed earlier. God is not concerned about controlling all this. There is also no Satan in Hindu philosophy misguiding the individual with his foreign hands. Man is at least free from such divine or extraterrestrial interference in his day-to-day life.

If man is free, can there be a destiny ?

Krishna exhorts Arjuna to fight, to decide his own destiny. This also means to exploit the possibilities of his destiny. In the theory of *karma* destiny does not mean that things are preordained. Destiny is what you arrive at. The individuals have their own options and compulsions. They may have an apparent choice of actions also. But no action can be in isolation. There would be billions of other factors, living and non-living, into the action fray also which cause each situation to be so peculiar and unique. They interplay. If one has a destiny, the others have a destiny too. Just as the final outcome is never based on the actions of one individual alone similarly there cannot be an individual isolated destiny. One's destiny depends not only on his own options but also on the options of others, and that is what makes destiny unpredictable and changeable.

That is what makes miracles a reality in life.

And where does the concept of luck stand? Luck may be something one is born with. But are we to associate only the riches with luck? Are other physical and mental talents not matters of luck? Is not the curiosity and capability to acquire knowledge and skill not matters of luck? Is not possession of the capacity to work hard, of the right attitudes which lead to success, the discrimination to recognise the right attitudes, the availability of such guidance to show the discrimination of right attitudes, the discrimination to recognise the right guidance also matters of luck? Where do we stop in our endeavour to define and limit the role of the divine (unknown) in the cosmic system?

In a way luck can be improved, it is said. The more and right people you know the better may be your luck. But then you must have the desire to succeed, the capability to recognise who should be cultivated, the perseverance to suffer and please such people, and again the luck to be accepted by such people. And all this may still not succeed when the hour of reckoning comes. It depends on the totality of the dynamics of the system.

Results can also be described as the end product of the dynamics of destinies. Destiny is only what you have in the end, not something that is predetermined or what is possible to predict. It is impossible to predict because, as Krishna says, it is impossible to unravel the mysteries of this cosmic design.

Future is not something ready, waiting to be unveiled. It is something getting manufactured every moment, by time, continuously. That is why it is impossible to predict what will happen. This is not to undermine science or astrology. These sciences study the patterns, the tendencies and hence predict possibilities. For example, if we have a mango seed we can say it may grow up into a tree, because the seed has that inherent potential, and hence the possibility. But whether it will actually happen cannot be known. That is destiny.

It all depends on how we decide to think. And we can decide to think as we want. We can rationalise the non-rational and find logic behind the lack of same. Believers of God may act as a matter of (blind) faith. But everyone can do it as a matter of a conscious and rational decision, for this alone can bring peace of mind. And peace so achieved is likely to be more enduring, as it would be based on a conscious and rational decision. Faith may breakdown, it may not fully convince ourselves, we might feel to be deluding ourselves on the strength of our faith.

Gita discusses the value of faith viz.a-viz. rational decision making , and we find Krishna telling Arjuna that those who are fully devoted to God are liked but those who act in a rationally detached way are better off. (XII 3-7) In any case beliefs/faiths do not alter the practical/material scene at all. In the final analysis the individual takes decisions based on his own inclinations (nature) only. And that is his *Karma.* Krishna tells Arjuna-

It is only your self-conceit that makes you say, "I will not fight"

Your resolution is vain, Because your true nature will compel you. (XVIII- 59)

In a way here Krishna is putting Arjuna in his proper place. Is it for Arjuna to decide whether he will fight in the battle or not ? Is he in control of his nature, his inclinations, his affections, his situation ? Is he trying to be the God ?

God and Indian Philosophy

The concept of a divine god is not fundamental to the Hindu philosophy. What do we mean by this word 'god'? Traditionally God is considered as a being or an entity, essentially having these qualities –

(a) an existence in the material sense,

(b) a sort of consciousness, and a desire to control and to take decisions,

(c) possession of some supernatural overwhelming power to effect decisions.

The first book of the Holy Bible is the Book of Genesis, which starts with the statement that in the beginning it was all dark and the world did not exist. And then Lord said let there be light and there was light and so the creation came into being by a powerful entity called god who pre-existed the creation and who took conscious decisions about working of this system and still does.

Since Hinduism is not an organized religion, not one founded by a code book, we can only go by what are the traditional practices and beliefs of Indians in ancient times. These beliefs of the common Hindu present a picture of a God not very different from the gods of other religions. But if we go by the fundamental philosophical treatises, the Vedas, the main Upanishads and Bhagavad Gita, then a very different picture emerges.

Rig-Veda is full of panegyric hymns venerating the numerous deities for their superhuman powers. Some scholars call it the prevalent polytheism. Actually none of these characters were in the category of a god. They were historical figures, like warlords who fought for the Aryans, and divine attributes got associated with them in time and legend. They lacked the status of absolute divinity. None of them was a supremo.

The sages of the Vedic age also came up with the concept of *Brahma,* a concept that should not be confused with god.

The Vedic scholars treated *Brahma* as the source of creation, not as the conscious creator. *Brahma* is not a creator in the sense that He was a powerful and conscious being who existed before the existence of the universe. *Brahma* was something from which the existence came out into being. *Brahma* was an entity possessed only with heat energy but was without consciousness or desires. Creation occurred out of *Brahma*, not by *Brahma*, and it occurred out of non-matter and without any external cause.

It is interesting to note that in Vedanta the stress is not on the worship of *Brahma* but on understanding of *Brahma*. In Bhagavad Gita, Krishna repeatedly says that when the *yogi* realizes that all this existence is just a variegated manifestation of *Brahma*, he assumes *sambhava*, and thus he integrates himself with *Brahma*, he attains the state of Brahma, a state of infinite peace and bliss. Thus *Brahma* is not a deity, it is not a god, it is nothing supernatural. *Brahma* is all that we are, and the abstract cause of all that is, it is a concept which has to be understood, realized and felt, not just to be worshipped.

And for this reason *Brahma* does not interfere or take decisions. *Brahma* is also not the chief controller of the human action. In Bhagavad Gita Krishna says that He does not take decisions into mundane human affairs, he does not interfere. Krishna says (Ch.V verses 14-15) that God creates neither the acts nor the cause nor the circumstances of the action. It is the nature that acts these out. God regards neither sin nor piousness.

Krishna further says that he is detached to whatever he is doing. He does not control the actions of people nor does he interfere with their affairs. Human actions neither affect him nor does he sit upon judgment on their lives. He does not take such decisions. He is not the grand judge. In fact there is no concept of a Day of Judgment in Hindu philosophy.

All works are accomplished by the qualities of nature. The ignorant feel they are the doer because of their ego. (Ch. III verses 27)

Though creator of this existence you should understand me as one who does not do anything (Ch. IV verses 13).

When one does not see the doer but sees only the qualities of nature performing their acts truly attains my being. (Ch. XIV verses 19)

The five factors which accomplish all actions are - the scene of action, i.e., the body, the doer, the instruments or the sensory organs or the faculties, the efforts, i.e., the motions or the impulses, and providence, i.e., the divine factors. (Ch. XVIII verses 14)

This is only to show that in Hindu philosophy there is no superman type of god who would actively intercede into human affairs, a concept normally regarded as divine, and linked to god. Since *Brahma* does not decide how the individual should act? Does anyone control ? Or are we all absolutely free ? Is all this uncontrolled and chaotic?

We cannot psychologically accept that it is all chaotic and haphazard. Scientifically also we do find some order in the scheme of things, some principles making things act in the way they do. Existences are not free to do anything they want. Krishna tells Arjuna that his resolve not to fight in the battle is vain and an offshoot of his ego. He tells Arjuna, 'You think you are going to take decisions. But no. Your own nature will compel you to fight.' Elsewhere also, Krishna says that even the sinner is a victim of his own nature, he is not a sinner in the real sense, as he is not the doer. Man is thus bound by his own nature in the context of his actions, but there is no extra-terrestrial control over him. This does put serious limitations on the individual's freedom but that is also true. It however relieves the individual from the dictates of an alien divine hand.

What is Nature ?

Nature is an abstract metaphysical force prevailing everywhere, in each entity, which causes the constituent factors to act in the way they do and hence is the cause of all actions. It is not that nature is something outside the material entity. Rather nature is an innate and inseparable part of the material entity.

It is that abstract factor which makes the material factor be or act whatever it is or does. And since it is an abstract quantity it can neither be fully understood nor completely controlled.

Nature controls everything, but it is a sort of non-predetermined control. What will be the outcome of the action is nowhere predetermined because all action that is taking place is a continuous process of interplay of the nature of various existences in an extremely dynamic and fluid situation. The process can be predicted to some an extent by empirical methods and by logic (the laws of science) but not always and not to the absolute exactness, both because of the sheer complexity of the total interaction and because of the unknown factors of nature.

Providence is also one of the factors of action, and this factor is unknown. No one can know this. It is mysterious. Like the uncertainty principle. We can understand a phenomenon on the basis of its principles but only to the extent of its singularity. There comes a point when the principle ceases to be applicable. That is its singularity stage. It is because of the principle itself is based on the phenomenon. Providence is not the divine but simply the unknown, the mysterious, the incalculable.

If one could calculate the behaviour and movement of every single atom of this existence then maybe one would be able to predict everything. Maybe not even then because the uncertainty principle holds that the very action of knowing something alters the motion and the position of that thing. As such by the time we come to know about it the thing has altered course.

'This three faceted Maya of mine is difficult to fathom.' (VII/14) Krishna does not expect man to be able to know fully the unknown facets of action.

Is there, then a god controlling things in this universe ? If we accept the phenomenon, then we have to *per se* also accept the concept of divine interference and divine disposition. But if we go by the theory of karmic burden and commiserate disposition, then the theory of nature acting upon the beings does not hold good. And if we believe in *Brahma* and the forces of nature then we cannot sustain the theory of the karmic burden of the previous life, or anything indicating divine dispensation.

Hindu philosophy was based on scientific perceptions, on rational and logical thought and there was little room in it for supernatural and divine concept of god. The philosophers believed in the concept of *Brahma* as the underlying universal cause of all existences. But the sages also realised that it was difficult for the common man to understand and accept such an abstract concept. To quote sh. 5 of Ch. XII of Gita:

Efforts are tremendous for those whose who cling to the formless one, because the path of formlessness is attained by mortal beings with great pain.

At the same time it was necessary not to break the simple belief in the divine of those people who were incapable of understanding a complex concept of *Brahma*. And so in the third chapter verses. 29 Krishna advises that the knowledgeable person should not confuse the simple minded one by his knowledge. Let the ordinary individual carry on with his simple faiths, or he will feel totally lost.

Law of *Karma*

Arjuna should know that the situation in which he has landed is not of his creation, that he cannot change either the situation or his position. He also cannot change his nature. If he decides not to fight, which may not be possible for him given his nature, even then he would not be at peace with himself. Can he be happy in a position where his brothers lose the battle because of his inaction? Can he suffer the ignominy of subjugation by the Kauravas ? Can he face defeat without fighting ? Will his nature let him do all this ?

The answer is obviously no. Arjuna is only temporarily swayed by the emotions of his attachments, which have clouded the reality of the total situation in which he actually is. Because of his sensory attachments he has lost the power of discernment to see through the reality of his own situation. Whether he likes or it dislike the situation is such which would compel him to fight. If he fights with a sense of guilt and remorse he will not be able to perform the duty of his situation well which will only add to his misery.

He knows that he is fighting for a rightful cause. So he is consciously not doing any crime or sin. If in the act anything wrong happens through his deeds he should regard it as an act of which he is only the instrument, not the conscious doer, and as such have no regret for it. As such he should fight, as a duty, without being affected by the consequences of his actions. Rather, he will have to fight. There is really no other option for Arjuna.

That is his *karma*.

9

EGO AND LIBERATION

There are occasions when one is in a dilemma. Occasions when one realises that there is something worldly/monetarily rewarding in a particular course of action. One also knows that he cannot follow that course of action because he is not like that. If he could have he would have. Who was stopping him? His self? Something in him? His nature? His conscience? Who was that? One must know that character.

Maybe one does not follow that ostensibly rewarding course of action because it is not in his nature to beg, or to kow tow the underlings and get pittance of their sops. Such alms would only annoy him. He also knows that by following his own sense of pride and self esteem, by refusing to bow he would at times be a loser in the worldly sense. He should know and be convinced about the fact that he is thus not a loser since he does not cherish such tainted results. He genuinely does not feel that such achievements, attained in this way are that important to him. It would not provide him the peace and happiness he is looking forward to. He would feel he is deceiving himself. So he would be happy in not pursuing such a course of action.

But if he really does cherish such goods, over and above his sense of self pride then his sense of self pride is a hypocrisy. One must know what he is, and must act accordingly. Peace and happiness thus depend in being true to oneself. Going against one's nature maybe of no good. One who understands himself is at liberty while the one who is bound by his complexes of ego is not. That is the relationship between ego and liberation.

The eleventh chapter of Gita is very interesting. In His endeavour to make Arjuna understand the cosmic system Krishna gives Arjuna a glimpse of His *Viraat-Roop*, a manifestation of His divine form. Arjuna is terrified and awed at this sight. He finds all human beings including his relatives, friends and enemies gradually drifting towards death (being swallowed by God). Krishna tells Arjuna that even if he does not fight in this battle all these men would die nevertheless (XII-32). In fact they are already dead and Arjuna is merely the instrument, the material cause, the apparent medium of the action of their death.

Death is the only absolute certainty of His system. And hence there is no point in lamenting or getting worried about it. It is better to accept it and to come to terms with it. Arjuna realises his own insignificance at this sight. When Arjuna had laid down his arms saying that he did not want to kill his relatives, he was under the delusion of the significance of his actions. He had thought that if he did not fight they would not die. His dilemma, his self-created delusion, as it was, his sense of guilt and remorse, emanated out of his ego. He thought he was to decide upon fate, and upon things over which he actually had no control. Arjuna's problem was that he was aware of his side only.

We all suffer from such parochial outlook. We think we know our problems whereas we actually see only the facade or the superficial part of the problem. That is often because we are unable raise ourselves above the immediacy/exigency of ourselves. Because of our attachments and personal concerns we often fail to put the problems in a right perspective. We get simply overwhelmed by the thoughts of the effects and thus ignore the basis of the cause.

The cause of the problems are usually only in the mind. We have problems because we are unable to adjust to or accept things we do not like/understand or feel apprehensive about. Strange things also threaten us. The problems are there only because things are not as we would like them to be. It is a problem only because we want the situation to be otherwise. Had we not wanted it otherwise it would not have been a problem in the first place.

We each also see a situation individually and hence often differently. We see things according to our own mindset, with our preconceived notions, through the filter of our extant value systems and in relation to our own context. Hence there can be no absolute evaluation of a situation of a problem. It can only be relative, in terms of the individual and his situation. Thus everything is contextual. Where we see a situation as a problem, at the same time others who are out of the situation see no problem at all.

Further, we feel we can change the situation, or should be able to change it but are annoyed at our own inability to do so. We also feel we are important enough for the situation to change itself to suit our requirements. Worst of all we want other living and thinking beings to act as we would like them to, and when this does not happen we feel unhappy. Thus we link our happiness to the actions of others, not to our own actions and thus we make ourselves slaves of others for our own happiness ourselves. Since the whole world cannot act in concert for our satisfaction we are likely to remain anxious and unsatisfied most of the time.

When we see a child crying for a balloon, or being happy just over some trifle possession we often say, 'Oh ! What a small world is it for the child. One balloon or a toy can make all the difference for him.' What we do not realise is that in the entire cosmic system, we are in an equally small world of ours'. In that cosmic scale our issues of concern, agony and happiness are as trivial or important as that of the child crying for a toy. But we are unable to place ourselves correctly in the cosmic context. That is to say that we do not realise our real position in the total context, at least we do not accept it.

We are in a state of anxiety, and tensions because we feel we can be in the charge of the situations but somehow we are not. We are psychologically not ready to accept this state of our inadequacy and insignificance in the world system. It hurts our ego.

Ego is a serious obstacle in the path to detachment as ego is a product of self-attachment. Most of our mental problems arise because we attach too much importance to ourselves, as if we are in charge of things we see, as if everything depends on us, as if we are the end of the world, as if we and hence our problems are immortal. We rarely view our problems in the backdrop of the transitory nature of everything. Of course it is hard to swallow that nothing human is really that important or eternal, but that is a truth. Once that is accepted the nature of involvement/ attachment to problems changes, the outlook changes.

We have already seen that in *Isha-Upanishad* it has been said that nothing belongs to the individual and hence there is no need for attachment or ego.

In Chapter II of Gita, Krishna had described Arjuna's resolve to abjure from the battle as unmanly, as an act of weakheartedness, which will bring disgrace ! Krishna had exhorted Arjuna to fight for glory and honour ! (Ch. II- verses 2 - 3) Later we find Krishna speaking against ego.

How do the two coexist - the concept of glory and lack of ego? Is this an anachronism, an inconsistency?

Actually there is no contradiction. Ego is the defense mechanism of our survival instinct, borne out of fear and weakness. One must realise ego as such. On the path of excellence, Ego is to be used as the power pack of the vehicle the steering of which is in the hands of the rational and unaffected (detached) mind. Thus the ego is used for accomplishing one's duties with distinction and with awareness of the same. What is not desirable however is the ego controlling the mind and thus the individual because then one cannot take rational decisions and one is likely to be led astray. It finally leads to inner conflicts and loss of peace of mind.

Then what is the value of ego?

In Upanishads also, freedom from Ego has been called as *Moksha,* the ultimate liberation. *Moksha* is not just freedom from the cycle of rebirths as traditionally often misunderstood by the religious minded people. It is simply the freedom from mental shackles on earth itself. It is the freedom from the bondage of works. It is not freedom from work but from their attachments. It is the freedom from the worries of its consequences. It is not a fatalistic resignation to an unknown quantity called destiny but a rational reprieve of the mind. We don't have to go out anywhere to achieve this salvation. It is an act to be done to our own self. That is through practice of *Yoga* and self-realisation.

The body and the senses, the faculties, have a utilitarian value and hence a purpose. The Self, as a part manifestation of the *Bramha* does not have any purpose and hence the mind has no rationale to get affected, and thus cannot/should not be controlled by ego. As Krishna says, God pervades in the individual Self and since God is detached/imbued with his own actions, there is no reason for the individual to be so attached. (Ch. XIII verses 31-32) This lack of attachment is liberation.

Chapter VI of Gita deals with the concept of having *sambhava,* the attitude of equivalence or sameness in everything. The *yogi* realises that everything and every being is nothing else but *Brahma* only. He himself is also *Brahma.* As such there is no reason to assume difference between individuals. The *yogi* sees everything in oneness with himself. That would be the end of ego.

Ego is nothing but attachment to oneself , and since attachment is illogical, ego is also illogical. (Ch. II verses 71) In fact emotion itself is an offshoot of self-importance, self attachment, and hence is illogical. That is why the *Yogi* treats pleasure and pain, victory and defeat with equal nonchalance. He ruthlessly follows the path of dharma (righteousness), which his conscience guides. He does his actions as his duty demands, and he is not swayed either by the desires of his senses of pleasure nor does he covet things for selfish gains. Thus he is free of his nature, of the actions caused by his nature, and of their result as well as of the affectations of the results of his actions.

He acts as if he is his own master. He has truly achieved liberation.

Gita also says that the wise/knowledgeable person should not confuse the ignorant. The most ignorant person is the one who is incapable of assessing another person's capacity/attitude for understanding. Thus if a person is incapable of transcending his mundane attachments, instead of giving him sermons one should try only to show him the path of peace through personal conduct, not by telling him that he stands condemned in the divine scheme. Nor should the wise feel himself superior for being in the know. One should take it as that both are equal, only they are different by way of nature. This will further liberate one from his complexes because one's own complexes are the real bonds of a person and each person has to find his own way of salvation.

There are no spiritual panaceas in Gita.

10

SOUL, SELF AND NATURE

The concepts of soul, transmigration and rebirth/after life have existed in many civilisations from time immemorial, in one form or the other. The ancient Egyptians and the Aryans believed in it and the civilisations of ancient Americans also indicate such beliefs. Even Pluto has written extensively on the concept of soul. From Rig-Veda to much later texts we find the concept being discussed in the Indian philosophy as well. How did this concept emerge in almost all civilisations ?

Just as the concept of God emerged out of man's failure to find any answer to his basic questions, so also the concept of an immortal eternal soul emerged out of man's refusal to reconcile with the phenomenon of inevitability and irreversibility of death. The instinct to survive needed a way out, an escape route. The concept of the immortal soul was a sort of consolation that even if the body dies there is something still left alive out of us. It is indeed difficult to accept a total death, to accept that on death absolutely nothing more is left out of our existence.

Soul and Gita

We know that there is yet no scientific proof of the existence of soul. Nor is there any about rebirth and such like things. What is the Gita's stand on the issue ?

At a time when completely negating the concept might have sounded as blasphemy Krishna puts both sides of the theory for the consideration of Arjuna. Although the few verses of Gita where the immortality of soul is spoken about are some of the most widely quoted ones but soul (as we often understand it) is neither the central theme nor the foundation/principal logic of the philosophy of Gita.

In the second chapter (verses 19 to 25) Krishna tells Arjuna that one should not mourn death because soul is immortal. Nothing can affect the soul and it remains pure and eternal. But immediately after this in the very next verse (26) Krishna adds that even if Arjuna does not believe in this concept of immortality of soul he should still not grieve death because death is certain and what is inevitable should not be grieved (worried) about ! After this the theme of soul is mentioned only scantily. Even in the few verses on the soul it is not said that we bear the burden of our previous lives or that we repay for our misdeeds in our next life (though some verses can be interpreted in that way).

We have to keep in mind that Gita was a product of its time. It certainly was not an original part of the Mahabharata. There is no trace of the teachings of Gita anywhere before the beginning of the battle of Kurukshetra. This feature of Bhagavad Gita is strongly cited as an indicator of the fact that Gita was a later addition to the Mahabharata. This is also evident from the fact that the gospel or the teachings of Gita are not mentioned in any of the later chapters of Mahabharata. Even at the end of the Mahabharata war the survivors go to Bhishma, the dying patriarch for knowledge. Nor do the teachings of Bhishma in that chapter contain the message of Gita.

Gita was an attempt to synthesise the philosophies of Upanishads and since the concept of immortal soul was strongly in vogue in certain schools of thought at that time it could not have been ignored in Gita. However by clarifying that one need not necessarily believe in soul for attaining peace and salvation, Gita transcends from the realm of a religious book to a treatise on rational and practical philosophy.

There is however the concept of a pure 'self', a part of the all pervading eternal *Brahma* residing in all beings. This self is not exactly the soul as we understand it. It is the metaphysical existence of the individual, above his material existence, and the concept helps the individual in introspection.

Self

Modern science, and psychology, today accept that an individual's personality is not a single compact linear unit. Instead, it is a combination of different components, in a dynamic state of flux. Genetic, environmental and psycho-somatic factors contribute to the making of the personality. There are many factors which are still unclear to science, particularly those related to the functioning of endocrine glands and the role of genetic code of the DNA (Deoxyribo-nucleic Acid).

Gita discusses the phenomenon of functioning of human mind by making clear distinctions amongst the self (soul), the body, the sensory faculties and nature. These factors interact and cause behaviour and action. In the earlier chapters we have seen how the philosophy of Gita treats the nature as an important function of human action. Gita says that nature is a separate force, which seriously affects the mind, the body and the senses, rather the entire human being. In fact it is the nature which is making the individual to act in the way he does. As such it is the nature, which is the doer/perpetrator of actions while the self or the soul is pure, aloof and unaffected. The affect of these internal forces is much more than the compulsions of the external factors.

What are the nuances of the distinction amongst Self (soul), Nature and the Body ? How does this force of nature operate on the individual ? What are the constituents of nature and how can the Self (soul) remain untouched by nature ?

In order to understand the 'Self' and the way nature operates we have to familiarise ourselves with the philosophical terms *prakrati* (nature) and *purusha* (person).

Prakrati and Purusha

The concepts of *prakrati* and *purusha* are very important to the philosophy of Gita. They are mainly dealt in the chapter XIII and explain how nature and body are related. The theory is essentially linked with the principle of nature of beings and leads to the concept of detachment. In fact it is the metaphysical logic of detachment, of being the non-doer.

This concept, of a pure and aloof self, away from the action doer within the individual (life-force) was first brought out beautifully in the Rig Veda in the following way.

Soul and consciousness like two friendly birds dwell together on this tree of existence. One of them, the consciousness, tastes the fruits while the other simply watches but does not savour anything. (I-164/20)

The same verse we find exactly repeated in *Shvetashvatara-Upanishad* (IV-6) and in *Mundaka-Upanishad* (3/1/1).

This was the first time when it was proposed that human personality constituted of a 'self' which is at a higher plane than the conscious and active life force. The concept was further elaborated later in *Shvetashvatara Upanishad* to explain how nature works upon the life-force itself, and becomes the cause of desires and preferences in the human mind and body.

Human personality is thus a dynamic system with forces, and compulsions, of body, senses, mind and nature that interact continuously causing thought and action to occur. Out of these forces, nature is the strongest. In fact, left uncontrolled it rules over the mind and the body.

Prakrati is usually translated as nature. Nature here is neither in the geographical sense nor is it confined to the way a person behaves. *Prakrati* is a non-conscious force which guides and moulds the human body and psyche. It is the cause of traits, tendencies and proclivities in the body and the mind of the individual. Nature however cannot act in vacuum. It needs an arena for operational activity.

This field of action for nature is the body in which, and through which, all the events take place. These are the events that occur through the birth, growth and the decline till the death of the body.

Purusha is the abstract person behind all these forces. He is the knower, the plougher of the field, i.e., body. It is the inactive and detached consciousness, which lies behind all the active states. In metaphysical terms, it is the pure and detached self.

The body being a live organism has essential requirements of the world. It is subject to sensory impulses and its consciousness. It is thus affected by these impulses. The body is called the field because it produces the harvest as the seeds are groomed in it. Thus the body has physical needs and desires. This field has its own constituents of construction and action. These are the sensory perceptions and understanding. Even the mental tendencies are a part of the field because they are objects of understanding and knowledge. And so the embodied soul has mental desires as well.

The body is not something debasing or sinful, because life does not exist without the body. Body is the field of action of nature, the instrument or the vehicle through which nature performs the action. It is also the abode of the self, a part of the imperishable *Brahma*. Thus proper maintenance of the body is not only unavoidable but also is a sacred duty. In fact Krishna is critical of those who indulge in severe acts of penance, which involve torturing the body. He says that by so tormenting the body they torment Him who dwells in the body. The essence is that nothing is obtained merely by self mortification either spiritually, intellectually or materially.

The body, the sensory organs and the mind are not separate or independent things. They are complimentary in a way, or part of the same thing that constitutes the human being. The way a body is built has a preponderate influence on one's psyche. It of course works the other way also. Mind/intellect may be only superior in hierarchy to the body or the sensory organs, but mind is not away from the total setup. It is a part of the setup. In Gita they all go together for the constitution of the field for the operation of nature. They are actually the faculties of the self, through which the self expresses itself in form of actions.

The body and the senses are produced by *prakrati* and the experience of pleasure and pain is suffered/ borne by the *purusha,* i.e., the self. Thus the field is the object and the knower is the subject. The Self however is like a mute witness. Since it does not need the material things for sustenance or survival (being the abstract principle) it remains unaffected. It is hence not the doer.

This can also be understood as the distinction between consciousness and the objects which that consciousness observes, as a witness. The witness here is not something physically residing in the body. It is also not any sub-conscious part of the human mind. It is also not just the voice of conscience. It is in the metaphysical sense the real self and does not need to use the senses or the mind for its witnessing. This is how the concept of self is different from the traditional concept of the immortal and transferable soul.

However there is no real duality between the two, i.e. between the body and the nature, which is acting on it. The cosmic process is an interaction between the two. The supreme power (forces of the cosmic system) is working on the field. The divine form *purusha* and the matter form *prakrati* belong to one spiritual whole, i.e., the *Brahma*. God's real being is veiled by the play of *prakrati* and its modes. As the self is part of that supreme being (God/*Brahma*) he cannot be a part of the affected acting field. The cosmic forces to which man is exposed represent the lower *prakrati*. *Purusha* is the pure supreme self.

Sambhava

The field, i.e., the body has its passing forms. The knower, the *purusha,* by development of moral qualities, without being attached, is no more confused by the passing forms of the body, or the material manifestations. Birth and death and all that goes in between appear to be mere outward events, which do not touch the eternity of the Self. And so the *yogi* maintains *sambhava*, i.e., sameness of attitude towards all situations and to all beings, realising that all this variation of beings and situations is just the facade created by the play of nature while behind this facade is the same *Brahma* everywhere. He is thus neither sad nor exultant.

The concept of *sambhava* is one of the greatest gifts of Indian philosophy to mankind. It was the precursor to the modern day terms of secularism and co-existence. *Sambhava* only means to have the sameness of feeling or attitude towards variation. The variation may be among men or situations. Variation being a part of nature is inevitable. Equality among men or sameness in any type of material forms is impossible in a dynamic cosmic system like the universe.

The *yogi* does not aspire for sameness of external forms. He simply views this variation as facets and manifestations of the same *Brahma*, which is everywhere and everything. Thus he adopts the same attitude towards all and sees no difference among the different. He knows that all these variations have been caused by the play of nature, otherwise behind this facade is the same *Brahma* everywhere. In Ch. V verse 18, Krishna says that the *yogi* sees the same *Brahma* in the Brahmin, the outcast, the cow and the dog.

This is not only a beautiful and philosophical logic for secularism, but also the most pragmatic way to adopt it socially. Societies and governments, which have tried to impose equality or uniformity from above have been found to be more oppressive than the phenomenon of inequality itself, and have eventually failed. One cannot be made taller by providing stilts. Secularism cannot mean denial or negation of difference. Social justice does not mean reversal of natural inequality. Doing so is impossible. Existence of differences has to be accepted without reservation or guilt.

What needs to be done is to develop a sameness of attitude, *sambhava*, so that the variation is seen without ego or other complexes, so that this variation does not create any inimical effect for the individual or for the society. Only such an attitude will bring true co-existence, social justice and secularism.

One must realise that all actions are being done by the *prakrati* and the *purusha* are free. This is the reason why the *Yogi* does not feel that he is the doer. It is the nature which is making the physical existence of the person to act in a particular way whereas the person himself (*purusha*) is not doing anything. In fact nature is even making the person think in the way he does. Rare is the person who can control his mind and rein his thoughts.

The saying 'Hate the sin not the sinner' is basically recognition of the fact that man is subject to nature, and can be a victim of his own tendencies. These tendencies may need correction, but the person himself should not be despised.

This perception of the Self can be attained by knowledge, it can be attained by meditation and also by detached action.

Whereas all beings are subject to forces of nature, in the hierarchy of species, the concept of 'self' must be unique to human beings. The earliest species of living beings had only a body, which had its own mechanism for its survival. During the course of evolution certain species developed sensory organs. These sensory organs were to help the body in its struggle for survival. Further development lead to the formation of a rudimentary brain, which again is a tool for survival. It coordinated between the sensory organs and the body for this purpose.

Development of an intricate intelligence system made *homo-sapiens* rulers of the earth. We declared ourselves as the supreme creation of God. Actually it was all a play of nature. Gradually in human beings mind became more powerful. It developed its own survival mechanism, and it made the body and the senses subservient to it. Today human body and the senses are being made to act so as to satisfy the needs of the mind instead of the other way round. However the forces of nature operating in the field, i.e., the body, are equally strong in human beings. And this dualism is the cause of dilemmas and mental confusions. This is because the mind also has the power of discrimination in the intelligence system. Man can realise, understand and even control nature to some extent. This discrimination is the cause of emergence/ presence of 'self' within man.

He who understands the self and the working of nature, and about the constituents of nature becomes free of the impulses and affects (results) of the nature. The one who perceives this distinction amongst the field, the knower and about the deliverance from nature attains the supreme state of integration with *Brahma*. In fact he attains *moksha* instantaneously even as he is alive.

One who is free of ego, attachment, guilt, remorse and all other types of emotions which can affect his mind is the most accomplished one, and hence the rare *yogi*. He is beyond the play of the forces of nature, because he feels that it is the nature which is causing actions while he (self) if away and thus free of the actions. He is not the doer.

This knowledge of oneself, about the interplay of *prakrati* and *purusha* leads to instantaneous liberation from all earthly bonds.

Having seen how nature acts in the field, that is the body, it is necessary to understand the constituents of nature, and how these constituents affect the thinking and the behaviour of the individuals. In fact it is the dominant constituent which decides the type of person one is.

Constituents of Nature

There is extensive deliberation in Gita about the qualities *(gunas)* or traits/tendencies in human beings. Since the basic objective of the discourse of Gita is to deliver man from his confusions and thus to bring him peace of mind Krishna explains the factors which create such confusions. Gita examines the traits in human nature which condition the thinking process of the individual and thus affect his mind. Krishna identifies three broad categories of constituents of nature of people— the *satvic,* the *rajasic* and the *tamasic.*

There is no human being who is free of these three qualities of nature, i.e., *Satva* (goodness), *Rajas* (passion) and *tamas* (darkness). All acts are influenced by these qualities.

The *satvic* person is pure and pursues the path of knowledge and attains peace and happiness.

The *rajasic* person is ruled by his cravings and greed. He is attached to his actions, which cause strife.

The *tamasic* person is ignorant, negligent, indolent and lazy.

The nature of these three types of persons is reflected in their actions, in their conduct and in the motives of actions. He who understands these constituents is a *yogi*. He remains unperturbed and detached, knowing that the disposition of nature is only the agent, the instrument, which is affecting the action.

However for such understanding and mental equilibrium proper control over the senses is essential. Krishna says that it is possible only for the *satvic* to achieve detachment and hence peace of mind, i.e., only the *satvic* can become a *yogi* . This is so because before one can attain that state one has to shed the scales of greed, pride, envy, lust, ego etc. The *yogic* type of lifestyle creates the environment where mind can think on the rational lines. If mind itself is clouded there can be no logical thinking.

It is desirable that one strives to achieve the stage of a *Yogi* because it is philosophically logical, rational in a holistic perspective and provides everlasting peace. Detachment is the key to achieve this state. And for that, the *satvic* mode of living, moderation, control over senses, knowledge, self-discipline and action for the good of others is conducive. Whereas the center of address is the individual (Arjuna) in Gita, the individual is not viewed in isolation. Gita always takes the individual in his social context.

Only the *satvic* mode of living is conducive to universal good, for it is in the interest of preservation and continuance of life. Man is a social animal and must know how to live in peaceful co-existence with others. It is thus instinctively closer to our nature to be good to others because only what is good for others can be good for us in the wider sense of the term. Anything else would only lead to conflict, strife and hence loss of peace of mind. Selfishness may finally prove to be self-destructive instead of being self-preserving. Those (the *rajasic* and the *tamasic*) who are concerned only about themselves, are controlled by their egos, and hence they cannot achieve the state of detachment and hence cannot find peace of mind for themselves or for others.

Thus the entire logic for living a pure and controlled life is based on reason, for the practical purpose of a peaceful and happy existence. It is not a divine edict but a very practical advice. The good is to be done not for appeasing any god because god does not absorb/accept/get affected by the sins or good turns (piety) of men. (Ch. V verse 14) The good is followed for one's own internal peace and satisfaction. And there is no happiness superior to the one achieved within oneself.

Krishna says that those who are discerning and achieve the state of being a *yogi* find salvation and peace of mind. However it is not so that others are condemned to a life of misery. By devotion and constant practice of a *satvic* (pure) way of life and by following one's nature one can find peace.

Thus *satva* becomes an essential step towards wisdom, towards *yoga*, towards achievement of the state of integration with *Brahma* which is the supreme *state,* and this is done by excelling in actions done without attachment and without desire of fruits of the actions.

11

THE *YOGI* MANAGER

This is an age of management excellence. We have managers, management consultants and management experts sprouting all over with their advises, theories and knowledge. There is a plethora of management institutes and management counsellors everywhere. Everyone seems to be having a view on how to manage, or how a manager should act. What do we look for in a good manager ? Let us list just a few of those qualities/management principles, and see if there is anything new we have not discussed about while discussing the philosophy of Gita.

These qualities/traits may be—

Diligence, excellence, ruthlessness, truthfulness, steadfastness, thoughtfulness, flexibility, decisiveness, confidence, rationality, fairness, social awareness, job satisfaction, productivity, objectivity, perseverance, capacity to withstand stress, generosity, etc.

The list may be unending and the priorities may vary depending upon the organisation and the situation. Now let us see how a follower of the principles of Gita fairs in this test of managerial capabilities.

Let us call him the *Yogi*-Manager.

The *Yogi* - Manager is a philosopher in action. To start with he is aware of the fact that he does not personally own the organisation or the world. Even if it is his own property he treats it as if he has been temporarily given the trust of it. (Mahatma Gandhi always exhorted the rich and the powerful to treat their money and position as a trust bestowed upon them by god for the general good).

The *Yogi*-Manager feels he is himself an outsider doing a job (being made to do the job by the system) for the sake of continuance of the world order (to keep the wheel of *Brahma* moving). He has no feeling of personal attachment or involvement in the act nor the notion of being the doer.

Thus he has no ego of his position. He knows that he is managing the works not because he is super intelligent or super efficient but only because the system (the cosmic order) has placed him (thrown him up) in his position, and now the system demands him to do the assigned job. Thus it is his duty to do it, and to do it well.

He uses his intelligence and capacity for hard work as instruments to fulfill the needs (commands) of the system which has provided him with the intellect and the capacity for work. He is not deluded by his powers of intellect or social authority. He does not suffer the complex of his capabilities. He knows that he is personally not to be credited for having such capacities. He has himself not done anything extraordinary to achieve these capabilities. It was nature working on him which made him develop so.

In fact he is humble about being in a position of power. He knows he could have been a born moron, a cripple or a midget. Just as the unfortunate individual with such handicaps is not personally to be blamed for such incapacities why should a person with inherent (god/nature given) gifts have the pride of possessing them ?

He accepts that the individual is as much a victim of his nature as of his situation. This develops a sense of empathy and humility in him. Yogi-Manager's this sense of humility makes him socially conscious, inside and outside the organisation. This helps him to improve his relations with his customers, staff and colleagues. He is best suited to handle industrial relations as people have faith in him. Such an atmosphere not only improves the working environment but ultimately leads to corporate efficiency. It also builds up the credibility of the management, and of the organisation as a whole. Everyone benefits out of it.

Yogi- Manager is dedicated towards his work. He loves to work. He works for work itself. He is self-motivated and needs no organisational awards to keep him working. He is enthusiastic about work because he enjoys doing his work. He works hard because he realises himself the fullest through action. He enjoys work because work gives him the opportunity for this self-actualisation. He puts his best in his job because he seeks happiness in his pursuit for excellence.

His work becomes efficient also because he takes all decisions with an unaffected and rational mind. He is not swayed by temporary impulses or emotions and hence always takes a thoughtful and balanced view of situations. This helps him in taking rational decisions. As he has no attachment he also has no prejudices or biases. He is objective in all decision making. He has nothing personal to gain out of his work.

He has the required sense of dedication and responsibility because he does his job as his fundamental duty. He is dependable. He can be fully relied upon. He needs no further supervision. He is his own overseer. In fact he feels himself the master of his work because he is working for his own satisfaction. He is working in a no-loss situation.

Because he has no selfish and ulterior motives of personal gain to pursue in his actions or decision making he wins the confidence and faith of others. He would be incorruptible. His customers, both internal and external, have confidence in his motives and decisions. His co-workers, juniors and colleagues like him because others know he works without prejudices or malice.

As he has no ego-hassles of his position or of being the doer (or owner) he is more amenable to reason. He is progressive and open minded. He is willing to listen to others as he does not regard himself as the end of knowledge and wisdom. He is forward looking as he has no recriminations of past. People find him humane and easier to work with. Such an approach not only helps him in taking more thoughtful decisions but others also feel involved in decision making and thus get committed to their decisions/ jobs. This further improves the corporate efficiency.

His efficiency is unaffected by the hierarchical structure of the organisation. He excels both in teamwork and in the position of leadership, for the two are the same to him. The problems of subordination do not touch him because he works like a master.

He is flexible in his approach. He is not dogged by his own earlier decisions. If he finds himself making a mistake he stands corrected without any sheepishness. He is willing for the tactical retreat, if necessary. He is ready and eager to review his own output objectively and without fear. He is enterprising because he has faith in himself and is not bogged down by fear of failure.

At the same time he is firm. He can even be ruthless. He is clear that what is to be done is to be done. He has objectives and duties, not motives. This makes him professional in work. He is business like but at the same time he is not unethical in his business decisions. He takes a holistic view of things and does not indulge in petty, parochial short sighted decision making. He has the courage to refuse to do what is not righteous or against the general good.

Above everything he is always cheerful and at peace. He takes his job as a sort of game to be played with all energy and talent, but with the knowledge that after all it is only a game. The stresses of the job do not affect him. He neither incurs nor generates tension because he is not working for himself. In fact he knows he is not working at all. He is not the doer. So no one is tense.

And at the end of the day he can have the last laugh, at himself , at life, at his work, at everything because he knows who he is.

He is the manager of tomorrow!

12

THE MAHABHARATA

Mahabharata is the longest poetical epic of the ancient times. It is also the richest piece of literature of the world. Said to have been originally composed more than a couple of thousand years back, it has also perhaps undergone a few modifications and additions in its form into what is now available to us. Bhagavad Gita is a very small part of this great epic. Though not entirely related in terms of its contents with the theme of the epic, it provides an interesting context for the discourse of Gita. As such it would be relevant to briefly recapture the storyline of Mahabharata.

Vichitra Virya, the King of Hastinapur, died young. His two wives gave birth to two sons. While Dhritarashtra was the elder one, he was born blind. As such, on coming of age, the younger one, Pandu, was asked to ascend the throne by his senior family members, as he was considered more suitable to be a king.

Pandu had five sons, called the Pandavas. Yudhishthira was the eldest and Arjuna was the third of these Pandavas. Dhritarashtra had a hundred sons called the Kauravas. Duryodhana was the eldest of the Kauravas. Pandu also met an early death. As his sons were too young to take over the reins of the kingdom, his elder Dhritarashtra was made the king regent, while the Pandavas and Kauravas continued with their education. The Pandavas and Kauravas grow up into great warriors. It was also the period when they developed intense rivalry and acrimony.

As the time passed, Duryodhana, who had developed aspirations to be the king himself, started conspiring to get rid of the Pandavas. When the time came for the eldest of the Pandavas, Yudhishthira, to ascend the throne Duryodhana invited the Pandavas to a game of dice where they were conned into losing everything. As a result it was decided that they would serve a period of thirteen years of exile in forests. The banished Pandavas underwent the ordeal but on return after the period was over, the Kauravas questioned their right to inherit the throne. Duryodhana was adamant that the Pandavas had forfeited their right of succession.

Dhritarashtra torn between the affection for his own children and the sense of righteousness was unable to decide either way. All efforts of mediation failed as Duryodhana was not willing to concede even a fraction of the kingdom to the Pandavas. The situation came to the crux that the issue could only be settled by the sword. The two camps prepared for the battle. They enlisted support of relatives and friendly neighbouring kings. The two armies came to the battlefield of Kurukshetra for the warfare.

As they are about to begin the fighting Arjuna is besieged with guilt and contrition at the thought of killing his own kinsmen and friends for the sake of kingdom. He feels remorse and refuses to enter into this warfare. Krishna, the king of Dwarka, is his charioteer. (Krishna is also one of the reincarnations of Lord Vishnu. Krishna considers such emotions on part of Arjuna as due to his ignorance of the cosmic system of the Supreme Being. He makes Arjuna understand the truth of the entire existence, of life, through a discourse which is called Shree Bhagavad Gita. On listening to this discourse Arjuna comes to terms with the realities of existence and of his own stead in the cosmic system. He realises his duty of the hour is to fight for his cause which is righteous and he enters the battle.

The battle of Mahabharata lasted for eighteen days in which the Kauravas were vanquished and slain and the Pandavas gained the kingdom of Hastinapur.

BHAGAVAD GITA

CHAPTER 1

The armies of Pandavas and Kauravas face each other at the battlefield of Kurukshetra. Arjuna requests Krishna to take his chariot close to the Kauravas so that he can have a look at the warriors he is set to fight. As the chariot is drawn closer to the enemy lines, Arjuna is overwhelmed at the sight of his cousins, relatives and friends among their ranks. He is stricken with guilt and remorse. Despondent at the prospect of killing his own kinsmen, Arjuna puts down his arms and tells Krishna that he cannot enter in this battle as it would be sinful to gain a kingdom which is obtained by killing ones' own relatives.

Dhritarashtra uvacha

Dharmakshetre kurukshetre samaveta yuyutsavah
mamakah pandavashchaiva kimakurvata sanjaya (1)

Dhritrashtra said- O Sanjaya, in Kurukshetra, the field of righteousness, what did Pandu's sons and my sons, gathered keen to fight, do ?

Sanjaya uvacha

Drishtva tu pandavanikam vyudham duryodhanastada
acharyamupasamgamya raja vachanamabraveet (2)

Sanjaya said- At that time, Prince Duryodhana saw the formation of Pandava's army and reaching near Guru Dronacharya thus addressed.

Pashyaitam panduputranam acharya mahatim chamum
vyudham drupadaputrena tava shishyena dhimata (3)

O Acharya, behold this massive army of Pandu's sons organised by your intelligent disciple Dhrishtadumna, son of Drupada.

Atra shura maheshvasa bhimarjunasama yudhi
yuyudhano viratashcha drupadashcha maharathah (4)

Dhrishtaketushchekitanah kashirajashcha viryavan
purujitkuntibhojashcha shaibyashcha narapungavah (5)

Yudhamanyushcha vikranta uttamaujashcha viryavan
saubhadro draupadeyashcha sarva eva maharathah (6)

Great archers and warriors are in this army who are equal to Bhima and Arjuna, like Satyaki, Virata, King Drupada, Dhrishtaketu, Chekitana, King of Kashi, Purujit, Kuntibhoja, Shaibya, Yudhamanyu, Uttamauja, Abhimanyu and the five sons of Draupadi, all of them are great warriors.

Asmakam tu vishishta ye tannibodha dvijottama
nayaka mum sainasya sangyartham taan bravimi te (7)

O best of Brahmanas, understand of those who are chief on our side. For your knowledge, I will name the commanders who are on our side.

Bhavan bhishmashcha karanshcha kripashcha samitimjayah
Ashvatthama Vikarnashcha Saumadattistathaiva cha (8)

Victorious warriors You Dronacharya, Bhishma, Karna, Kripacharya, Ashvatthama, Vikarna and Bhurishrava, son of Somadatta.

Anye cha bahavaha shura madarthe tyaktajivitah
nanashastrapraharanah sarve yuddhavisharadah (9)

And many other bravemen who have put their lives at stake for me, warriors armed with different types of weapons, all proficient in warfare.

Aparyaptam tadasmakam balam bhishmabhirakshitam
paryaptam tvidametesham balam bhimabhirakshitam (10)

Our army protected by Bheeshmapitamah is invincible and their army, protected by Bheema, is vulnerable.

Ayaneshu cha sarveshu yathabhagam avasthitah
bhishmam evabhirakshantu bhavantah sarva eva hi (11)

As such you all must strongly defend Bheeshma from the front in your ranks from all directions.

Tasya sanjanayan harsam kuruvraddhah pitamaha
sinhanadam vinadyochchaih
shankham dadhmau pratapavan (12)

Then the elder among the Kurus, valiant Bhishma roaring like a lion, blew the conch shell heartening up his grandson Duryodhana.

Tatah shankhashcha bheryashcha panavanakagomukhah
sahasaivabhyahanyanta sa sabdas tumuloabhavat (13)

After that, conches, drums cymbals, trumpets blew up together echoing in a tremendous crescendo.

Tatah shvetaiharyairyukte mahati syandane sthitau
madhavah pandavashchaiva divyau shankau
pradadhmatuh (14)

Then Krishna and Arjuna, sitting in their fine chariot of white horses, also blew their celestial conches.

Panchajanyam rishikesho devadattam dhananjayah
paundram dadhmau mahasankham bhimakarma
vrkodarah (15)

Krishna sounded his panchajanya, Arjuna his Devadatta and Bheemasenas his Paundra.

Anantavijayam raja kuntiputro yudhishthirah
nakulah sahadevashcha sughoshamanipushpakau (16)

King Yudhishthira sounded his Anantavijaya named conch as did Nakula and Sahadeva blowing Sughosha and manipushpaka respectively.

Kashyashcha paramesvasah shikhandi cha maharathah
dhrashtadyumno viratashcha saatyakishcha parajitah (17)

Drupado draupadeyashcha sarvashah prthivipatey
saubhadrashcha mahabahu shankhan dadhmuh
prithakprithak (18)

The King of Kashi, warriors Shikhandi and Drashtadyumna, King Viraat and the invincible Saatyaki, King Drupada , the five sons of Draupadi and Abhimanyu also blew their conches.

Sa ghosho dhartarashtranam hridayani vyadarayat
nabhashcha prithivim chaiva tumulo vyanunadayan (19)

These tremendous sounds, reverberating through the earth and the sky shook the hearts of the Kauravas.

Atha vyavasthitan drashtva dhartarashtran kapidhvajah
pravartey shastrasampatey dhanurudyamya
pandavah (20)

Rishikesham tada vakyamidamaah mahipatey
senayorubhayormadhye ratham sthapaya me achyuta (21)

O King ! Watching the relatives of Dhritarashtra in battle formation, picking up his bow for preparing to launch weapons, thus spoke Arjuna to Krishna O Achyuta ! Park my chariot in the middle of the two armies.

Yavadetanniriksheyaham yoddhukamanavasthitan
kairmaya saha yauddhavyamasmin ranasamudyamey (22)

And keep the chariot standing there till I have seen clearly those opponent warriors with whom it is appropriate for me to fight.

Yotsyamananavekshey aham ya eteyatra samagatah
dhartarashtrasya durbuddheryuddhey
priyachikirshavah(23)

I would like to see all those kings who have come to this battle in support of the crooked minded Duryodhana.

Sanjaya uvacha

Evamukto rishikesho gudakeshena bharata
senayorubhayormadhye sthapayitva rathottamam (24)
Bhishmadronapramukhatah sarvesam cha mahikshitam
uvacha partha pashyaitan samavetan kuruniti (25)

Sanjaya said— O Dhritarashtra, on these words of Arjuna, Shri Krishna brought the chariot in the middle of the two armies in front of Bhishms and Dronacharya and all other kings, and said-O Arjuna! Have a look at the Kauravas who are set to battle against you."

Tatrapashyatisthitan parthah pitranatha pitamahan
aacharyan matulan bhratrin putran pautran
sakhimstatha (26)

Shvashuran suhradashchaiva senayorubhayorapi
tan samikshya sa kaunteyah sarvan bandhun
avasthitan (27)

Kripaya parayavishto vishidannidamabaraveet
drashtvemam svajanam krishna yuyutsum
samupasthitam (28)

Sidanti mam gatrani mukham cha parishushyati
vepathushcha sharirey may romaharshascha jayate (29)

There Arjuna saw fathers and grandfathers, sons and grandsons, uncles, relatives, teachers and friends. Also were fathers-in-law on both the sides.

Seeing all relatives thus standing Arjuna, son of Kunti was overwhelmed with contrition and spoke with sadness to Krishna,

"O Krishna, the sight of assembled my own people eager to fight in this battlefield makes me tremble. My mouth gets dry and my limbs shiver.

Gandivam sransate hastatvakchaiva paridahyatey
na cha shaknomyavasthatum bhramativa cha me
manah (30)

My bow Gandiva slips from my hands and I feel my skin is burning. My mind is confused and I am unable to stand.

Nimittani cha pashyami viparitani keshava
na cha shreyo anupashyami hatva svajanam ahave (31)

O Krishna ! I can see only ominous portents in this, and I do not see any benediction in the killing my own men in this battle.

Na kangkshey vijayam krishna na cha rajayam
sukhani cha
kim no rajyena govinda kim bhogair jivitena va (32)

O Krishna I neither want victory nor the kingdom nor the pleasures. What is our purpose for such a kingdom or for such pleasures, and also what good is such a life for.

Yesham arthe kangkshitam no rajyam bhogah sukhani cha
ta ime avasthita yuddhe pranams tyaktva dhanani cha (33)

They, for whom we want the kingdom and its pleasures are themselves standing here resigning their lives and riches.

Aacharyah pitarah putrastathaiva cha pitamahah
matulah shvashurah pautrah shyalah
sambandhinastatha (34)

Etaana hantum ichchami ghnato api madhusudana
api trailokyarajyasya hetoh kim nu mahikrtey (35)

Also are teachers, uncles, boys, as also in-laws, grandsons and other relatives. I would not like to kill them even for the reign of the three worlds, what to say for the earth.

Nihatya dhartarashtran nah ka pritih syajjanardana
papam evashrayedasman hatvaitan atatayinah (36)

What happiness will we get in killing the sons of Dhritarashtra ? We will only incur sin by killing these predators.

Tasman narha vayam hantum dhartarashtran svabandhavan
svajanam hi katham hatva sukhinah syama madhava (37)

As such O Madhava ! We do not deserve to kill our own brothers, the sons of Dhritarashtra, because how can we be happy on killing our own family members ?

Yadyapyete na pashyanti lobhopahatachetasah
kulakshayakritam dosham mitradrohe cha patakam (38)

Katham na jneyamasmabhih papadasmannivartitum
kulakshayakritam dosham prapashyadbhir janardana (39)

Although these corrupted people do not find anything wrong in destroying the family and sin in contesting their friends, nevertheless, why we, who are aware of the blunder of destroying the clan, should not think of getting out of committing this sin, O Krishna.

Kulakshaye pranashyanti kuladharmah sanatanah
adharme nashte kulam kritsnam adharmoabhibhavatyuta (40)

If the clan is ruined the traditional values are destroyed, and its loss deprives the clan of all sense of righteousness.

Adharmabhibhavat krishna pradushyanti kulastriyah
strishu dushtasu varshneya jayatey varnasankarah (41)

O Krishna ! Rise of sin corrupts the women of the family, which jeopardises the whole social structure.

Sankaro narakayaiva kulaghnanam kulasya cha
patanti pitaro hyesam luptapindodaka kriyah (42)

Such an anarchy leads the clan, and also those who ruin it to hell. It even affects the spirits of the ancestors.

Doshairetaih kulaghnanam varnasankarakarakaih
utsaddyantey jatidharmah kuladharmash cha shashvatah (43)

Through these evils bringing about caste mixture the age long caste-traditions and family customs of the massacres of relatives get extinct.

Utsannakuladharmanam manushyanam janardana
narakeaniyatam vaso bhavatityanushushruma (44)

O Janardana ! It is said that those who have lost the family values stand condemned to hell forever.

Aho bata mahatpapam kartum vyavasita vayam
yadrajyasukhalobhena hantum svajanamuddyatah (45)

Alas! What a tragedy that for the greed of kingdom and pleasures, we despite being intelligent people, have become frenetic enough to commit this sin of killing our own people.

Yadi mam apratikaram shastram shastrapanayah
dhartarashtra rane hanyustanme kshemataram bhavet (46)

Even if the sons of Dhritarashtra kill me in my state of disarm and defencelessness, it would be better for me to die so.

Sanjaya uvacha

Evamuktvarjunah sankhye rathopastha upavishat
visrajya sasharam chapam shokasanvignamanasah (47)

Sanjaya said - Having spoken so in the battlefield, distressed and sad, Arjuna discarded the bow and the arrow and sat in the rear part of the chariot.

CHAPTER II

Shri Krishna rebukes Arjuna for his despondency and calls it as his faintheartedness and his conduct as unbecoming of a warrior. He explains that since soul is immortal, and since death is inevitable, it is unwise to grieve for death. He exhorts Arjuna to enter the battle as his duty, treating victory and defeat alike, because he has control only over his actions not over their outcome. Freedom from bondage of work is obtained by discarding attachment to the results from ones' actions. And hence he should only concentrate on the actions his duty demands, not over the consequences, and treat success and failure alike, as they are not within the realm of his determination.

This state of mental stability requires control over mind and senses.

The senses go after their cravings. They are a part of the human chemistry. One should understand and control them, in the sense that one should not be driven by them. Mere physical abstemious attitude is not all. One should have that control in the mind and in the attitudes.

Sanjaya uvacha

Tam tatha kripayavishtam ashrupurnakulekshanam
vishidantamidam vakyam uvacha madhusudanah (1)

Sanjaya said - To Arjuna who was grief stricken, distressed and full of pity and tears, thus spake Bhagawan Madhusudana.

Shri Bhagavan uvacha

Kutastva kashmalamidam vishame samupasthitam
anarya jushtama asvargyam akirtikaram arjuna (2)

Shri Bhagawan said -

How come you developed this desire at this dark hour ? This attitude is unbecoming of great men. It leads neither to heaven nor to glory.

Klaibyam ma sma gamah partha naitattvayyupapadyate
kshudram hridayadaurbalyam tyaktvottistha
paramtapa (3)

As such Arjuna ! Do not be so unmanly Arjuna. It does not befit you. O great warrior ! Get rid of this petty faintheartedness and prepare for the battle.

Arjuna uvacha

Katham bhishmam aham sankhye
dronam cha madhusudana
ishubhih pratiyotsyami pujarhavarisudana (4)

Arjuna said- O Madhusudana, how do I fight Bheeshma and Dronacharya on the battlefield with arrows ? They are both worthy of reverence.

Gurun ahatva hi mahanubhavan shreyo bhoktum
bhaikshyam apiha lokey
hatvartha kamanstu gurunihaiva bhunjiya
bhogan rudhirapradigdhan (5)

I consider it is better to live on alms than to kill these great teachers because after killing them the wealth and the pleasures I would be having would bear stains of their blood.

Na chaitadvidamah kataranno gariyo yadva jayema yadi
va no jayeyuh
yaneva hatva na jijivishamaste avasthitah pramukhe
dhartaràstrah (6)

We do not even know what is good for us, to fight or not to, or who will be the victor. And those without whom life is not worth living, our cousins the sons of Dhritarashtra, are here confronting us in the battlefield.

Karpanyadoshopahatasasvabhavah prchchami
tvam dharmasammudhachetah
yachchreyah syannichshitam bruhi tanme shisyaste
aham shadhi mam tvam prapannam (7)

Stung by cowardice and confused about what is righteousness (eternal relationship between the creator and the creatures), I ask you what is good for me. Being under your shelter, please enlighten me.

Na hi prapashyami mamapanudyayachchokamu-
chchoshanam indriyanam
avapya bhumav asa patnamddham rajyam
suranamapi chadhipatyam (8)

Because even if I conquer worldly powers and opulent lands I do not find anything which would drive out the pain from my senses.

Sanjaya uvacha

Evamuktva rishikesham gudakeshah paramtapa
na yotsya iti govindamuktva tooshnim babhuva ha (9)

Sanjaya said -O King, mighty Arjuna told omniscient God Krishna, "I shall not fight," and saying so became absolutely silent.

Tam uvacha rishikeshah prahasanniva bharata
senayorubhayor madhye vishidantamidam vachah (10)

O Dhritarashtra ! Then so spoke omnipresent Shri Krishna, smiling towards the grieving Arjuna betwixt the two armies, i.e., the armies of Kauravas and Pandavas.

Shri Bhagavan uvacha

Ashochyannvashochas tvam pragyavadamshcha bhashase
gatasunagatasumshcha nanushochanti panditah (11)

Shri Bhagawan Krishna said -O Arjuna, you grieve for those who beings who need not be grieved about and you speak like a wise man. But the intelligentsia grieve neither for the living nor for the dead.

Na tvevaham jatu nasam na tvam neme janadhipah
na chaiva na bhavishyamah sarve vayamatah param (12)

In fact, there was never a time when I did not exist, or you and the nobles were not here, nor will there ever be a time when we all will not be.

Dehino asmin yatha dehe kaumaram yauvanam jara
tatha dehantara praptir dhirastatra na muhyati (13)

Just as the soul passes through the stages of childhood, youth and age in the body, so does it assume a new body. The steadfast person is not affected by this process.

Matrasparshastu kaunteya shitoshna sukhaduhkhadah
agamapayinoanityastamstitikshasva bharata (14)

O son of Kunti, sensations of cold and warmth, of pleasure and pain, are ephemeral. As such, learn to bear with them.

Yam hi na vyathayantyete purusham purusharshabha
samaduhkhasukham dhiram soamratatvaya kalpate (15)

Because, one who treats pleasure and pain alike is not tormented by the impulses of the senses, he deserves salvation.

Nasato vidyate bhavo nabhavo vidyate satah
ubhayorapi drashtoantasnatva anayostattava
darshibhih (16)

What does not exist does not matter, and there is no end to the existence. The wise people see the essence of the both.

Avinashi tu tadviddhi yena sarvamidam tatam
vinashamavyayasyasya na kashchit kartum arhati (17)

You should consider as indestructible only that whose immanence is everywhere in existence. No one can destroy that indestructible (brahma).

Antavanta ime deha nityasyoktahháririnah
anashino aprameyasya tasmadyu dhyasva bharata (18)

O Arjuna All these bodies (manifestations) of the eternal indestructible soul are destructible. As such you must fight.

Ya enam vetti hantaram yashchainam manyate hatam
ubhau tau na vijanito nayam hanti na hanyate (19)

Those who think that this soul can kill or that it can die do not understand the soul because it can neither kill nor can it be killed.

Na jayate mriyate va kadachinnayam bhutva
bhavita va na bhuyah
ajo nityah shashvato ayam purano na hanyate
hanyamane sharirey (20)

This eternal soul is never born nor does it ever die, because it is constant, eternal, ancient ant without origin. It does not die even after the body dies.

Veda vinashinam nityam ya enamajam avyayam
katham sa purushah partha kam ghatayati hanti kam (21)

O Arjuna, if one who considers the soul as unborn, indestructible, inehaustible and eternal, how does he kill anyone or get anyone killed ?

Vasamsi jirnani yatha vihaya navani grahnati naro aparani
tatha sharirani vihaya jirnanyanyani
sanyati navani dehi (22)

Just as a person discards the old clothes and puts on new ones, similarly the soul gives up the old body and assumes a new ones.

Nainam chchindanti shastrani nainam dahati pavakah
na chainam kledayantyapo na shoshayati marutah (23)

Weapons cannot pierce this soul, fire cannot burn it, water cannot dissolve (or wet) it, and the wind cannot dry it.

Achcheddyo ayam adahyo ayam akleddyo ashoshya eva cha
nityah sarvagatah sthanur achalo ayam sanatanah (24)

This soul is unpenetrable, it is incombustible, it is steadfast, omnipresent, eternal and ever the same.

Avyakto ayamachintyo ayam avikaryo ayamuchyate
tasmadevam viditvainam nanushochitum arhasi (25)

This soul is unrevealed, uncomprehensible and is not vulnerable. Knowing the soul as such you should not grieve.

Atha chainam nityajatam nityam va manyase mratam
tathapi tvam mahabaho naivam shochitumarhasi (26)

Jatasya hi dhruvo mrityurdhruvam janma mritasya cha
tasmadapariharye arthe na tvam shochitumarhasi (27)

Even if you believe that soul is subject to birth and death, still you do not deserve to grieve like this because according to this belief, death is certain for one who is born, and since there is no remedy to it, you need not grieve for it (what is inevitable).

Avyaktadini bhutani vyaktamadhyani bharata
avyaktanidhananyeva tatra ka paridevana (28)

All living beings are visible only between the period of birth and death. They were not so before birth nor will be after death. Then why this grief ?

Ascharyavatpashyati kashchidenam
ashcharyavadvadati tathaiva chanyah
ashcharyavachchaina manyah shranoti
shrutvapyenam veda na chaiva kashchit (29)

Only some gifted person may discern this soul, and rarely may one describe its essence as a wonder, or hear about it, and still one may not understand it.

Dehi nityamavadhyoyam dehe sarvasya bharata
tasmat sarvani bhutani na tvam shochitum arhasi (30)

This soul inside every person's body is never assailable, and so you should not lament for the entire mankind.

Svadharmamapi chavekshya na vikampitumarhasi
dharmyaddhi yuddhachchreyo anyat
kshatriyasya na vidyate (31)

Nor should you fear the call of your duty as no duty is more sacrosanct as that of a battle for a warrior.

Yadrachchaya chopapannam svarga dvaram apavratam
sukhinah kshatriyah partha labhante
yuddhamidrasham (32)

Only the lucky warriors find the gates of heaven so open for them, in the form of such a battle.

Atha chettvamimam dharmyam sangramam na karishyasi
tatah svadharmam kirtim cha hitva papamavapsyasi (33)

But if you do not fight this sacred battle, you shall forfeit your creed and glory and shall attain sin.

Akirtim chapi bhutani kathayishyanti te avyayam
sambhavitasya cha kirtirmaranadti richyate (34)

People will talk of your inglory for ages, and infamy is worse than death for an honourable man.

Bhayadranaduparantam mansyante tvam maharathah
yesham cha tvam bahumato bhutva yasyasi laghavam (35)

You shall stand belittled by those who held you high in esteem, for they will ascribe your withdrawl as due to fear.

Avachya vadanshcha bahun vadishyanti tavahitah
nindantastava samarthyam tato duhkhataram nu kim (36)

Your rivals, disparaging your might, would say many demeaning things about you. What would be more tragic ?

Hato va prapsyasi svargam jitva va bhokshyase mahim
tasmaduttishtha kaunteya yuddhaya kratanishchayah (37)

Either you will die in the battle and achieve heaven or you will win the battle and enjoy the kingdom. As such Arjuna, stand up and be determined to fight.

Sukhadukhe same kratva labhalabho jaya jayao
tato yuddhaya yujyasva naivam papamavapsyasi (38)

Consider victory and defeat, loss and gain, pleasure and pain alike and prepare for the battle. So battling, you shall incur no sin.

Esha te abhihita sankhye buddhiryoge tvimam shranu
buddhya yukto yaya partha karmabandham
prahasyasi (39)

This is the wisdom of transcendental/Knowledge *(Sankhya)*. Now heed to the wisdom of Action *(Karma-yoga)* with which also you can deliver yourself out of the bondage of actions.

Nehabhikramanasho asti pratyavayo na vidyate
svalpamapyasya dharmasya trayate mahato bhayat (40)

In this path of karma yoga, no effort is lost and there are no adverse repercussions. Even a little practice of this wisdom saves you from the fear of birth and death.

Vyavasayatmika buddhirekeha kurunandana
bahushakha hyanantashacha buddhayo avyavasayinam (41)

Those resolute in this wisdom think straight. The mind of the greedy goes on various tracks.

Yamimam pushpitam vacham pravadantyvipashchitah
vedavadaratah partha nanyadastiti vadinah (42)

Kamatmanah svargapara janamkarmaphalapradam
kriyavishesha bahulam bhogaishvarya gatim prati (43)

Bhogaishvarya prasaktanam tayapahrata chetasam
vyavasayatmika buddhih samadhau na vidhiyate (44)

Those who are involved in consumption, who love only those parts of Vedas which glorify attainment as a result of birth and work alone, who feel heaven is everything, who love power and pleasure and who follow rituals for such ends, such injudicious persons are not intellectually resolved towards such wisdom of self (introspection).

Traigunya vishaya veda nistraigunyo bhavarjuna
nirdvandvo nityasattvastho niryogakshema atmavan (45)

Let not the issues of the three traits dealt in the Vedas affect you. You should be internally independent and free of the dualism of grief and happiness.

Yavanartha udapane sarvatah samplutodake
tavan sarveshu vedeshu brahmanasya vijanatah (46)

One who understands the essence of bramha has little use of Vedas.

Karmanyev adhikarste ma phaleshu kadachana
ma karmaphalahetur bhurma te sango astva karmani (47)

You control only your actions, never the consequenses. As such do not become the cause of the results of the actions, nor be disposed towards inaction.

Yogasthah kuru karmani sangam tyakatva dhananjaya
siddhya siddhyo samo bhutva samatvam yoga uchyate (48)

Discarding attachments (to the results of the action), be steadfast in yoga and treat success and failure alike with equanimity. Yoga is being of uniform mind in all situations.

Durena hyavaram karma buddhiyoga dhananjaya
buddhau saranam anvichcha kripanah phalahetavah (49)

Those who go after fruits of action are indeed poor. Such actions are also inferior. As such you must persue what is of wisdom.

Buddhiyukto jahatiha ubhe sukrtadushkrte
tasmaddyogaye yujyasva yogah karmasu kaushalam (50)

Man with uniform mind is liberated from actions, both good and evil. As such devote yourself to yoga, which is excellence in work as well as freedom from the bondage of works.

Karmajam buddhiyukta hi phalam tyaktva manishinah
janmabandha vinirmuktah padam gachchantya namayam (51)

With undistracted mind one is liberated from the bonds of life as he detaches himself from the fruits of action. Thus he achieves the supreme state.

Yada te mohakalilam buddhir vyatitarishyati
tada gantasi nirvedam shrotavyasya shrutasya cha (52)

Once you are able to overcome the allurements you will develop a disinterest towards things you hear of.

Shrutivipratipanna te yada sthasyati nishchala
samadhavachala buddhistada yogam avapsyasi (53)

Your distracted mind when concentrated and stable will achieve the state of yoga.

Arjuna uvacha

Sthita pragyasya ka bhashsa samadhisthasya keshava
sthitadhih kim prabhasheta kimaseet vrajeta kim (54)

Arjuna asked- O Krishna, what are the signs of a person with a stable mind ?

Shribhagavan uvacha

Prajahați yada kaman sarvan partha manogatan
atmanyevatmana tushtah sthitapragyasta dochyate (55)

Lord Krishna said- When man gives up all desires and is content in his self then he is said to be one of stable mind.

Duhkheshvanu dvignamanah sukheshu vigatasprhah
vitaragabhayakrodhah sthitadhir muniruchyate (56)

For whom grief causes no consternation, who is unconcerned about getting pleasures and who has no fear, anger and complexes, such a person is said to be one of a stable mind.

Yah sarvatran abhi snehas tat tat prapya subhashubham
nabhi nandati na dveshti tasya pragya pratishthita (57)

One who is always unaffected and who neither rejoices nor loathes anything, such a person is said to be one with stable mind.

Yada sanharate chayam kurmo anganiva sarvashah
indriyani indriyarthebhyastasya pragya pratishthita (58)

When the person withdraws his senses from sensations, like a tortoise withdrawing its limbs into its shell, then his mind becomes stable.

Vishaya vinivartante niraharasya dehinah
rasavarjam raso apasya param drishtva nivartatey (59)

By deprivation one does abstain from sensations but the cravings still remain. Only Supreme blessing relieves the stable mind of the cravings, (i.e., it is difficult to achieve or it is a matter of luck).

Yatato hyapi kaunteya purushasya vipashchitah
indriyani pramathini haranti prasabham manah (60)

Turbulent by nature, the senses even of a wise person, who is practising self-control, forcibly carry away his mind, Arjuna.

Tani sarvani sanyamya yukta aaseet matparah
vashe hi yasye indriyani tasya pragya pratishthita (61)

Only the person who can control his senses can have a stable mind. As such one should rein his senses and be steadfast in devotion to me.

Dhyayato vishayan punsah sangasteshu pajayate
sangatsanjayate kamah kamat krodho abhijayate (62)

Senses lead to attractions and develop desires. Non-fulfillment of desires leads to anger.

Krodhad bhavati sammohah sammohat smriti vibhramah
smriti bhranshad buddhinasho
buddhinashat pranashyati (63)

Anger distorts discernment and causes loss of memory. This affects the intellectual knowledge and loss of intellect causes downfall of the individual.

Raga dvesh viyukttaistu vishayani indriyaishcharan
atmavashyair vidheyatma prasadam adhigachchati (64)

One who keeps the senses under control, remains free of attraction or aversion. Even as he uses his senses (for worldly activities) he remains in internal bliss (free of their affectations).

Prasade sarvaduhkhanam hanirasyo pajayate
prasannachetaso hyashu buddhih paryavatisthate (65)

Internal bliss removes all sorrows and gives stability of mind.

Nasti buddhir ayuktasya na chayuktasya bhavana
na chabhavayatah shantir ashantasya
kutah sukham (66)

Uncontrolled senses cause instability of mind. Unstable mind is internally unsure. Such a person is never at peace and how can there be happiness without peace ?

Indriyanam hi charatam yanmo anu vidhiyate
tadasya harati pragyam vayur navami vambhasi (67)

Just as winds carry away the sail-boat so do the senses carry away the intellect.

Tasmadyasya mahabaho nigrahitani sarvashah
indriyani indriyarthe abhyastasya pragya pratishthita (68)

He who withdraws his senses from their objects of their cravings attains a stable mind.

Ya nisha sarvabhutanam tasyam jagarti sanyami
yasyam jagrati bhutani sa nisha pashyato muneh (69)

What is like a dark night to others is daylight for the wise man, and when (where) others are awake the wise man is asleep (unaffected).

Apuryamanam achala pratistham samudramapah
pravishanti yadvat
tadvat kama yam pravishanti servey
sa shantimapnoti na kamakami (70)

Just as the ocean remains calm even as it absorbs the various rivers so does the steadfast person remain calm even as all his desires are fulfilled. One who craves for fulfillment of desires never gets peace.

Vihaya kamanyah sarvanpu mamshcharati nihsprhah
nirmamo nirahankarah sa shantimadhi gachchati (71)

He who gives up all desires, and acts without pathos, ego or longing attains peace.

Esha brahmi sthitih partha nainam prapya vimuhyati
sthitva syamanta kale api brahma nirvanamrachchati (72)

O Arjuna! Thus is the state of the person who realises bramha. Attaining this divine state he is never deluded and at last achieves the divine bliss.

CHAPTER III

Krishna tells Arjuna that freedom from bondage of work is not attained by renunciation or abdication. Action is unavoidable. One has to sustain life and act for it, almost helplessly, guided by the compulsions of nature. So the wise person, the yogi, continues to do his assigned work as a duty, but without any attachment to the work or its results, as if it is a sacrifice. He performs his duties for the sake of maintenance of the world order, without the interest of gain from the actions, and remains content with himself. Krishna further adds that even He has nothing to gain from His work but He continues to work because it is his duty, for keeping the world moving.

Attachment is a sign of ignorance because it is always the natural course of action which is taking its path. We who are misguided by our ego feel that we are doing all this. The knowledgeable person understands that all actions are a part of the dynamics of the cosmic system, and he is thus free from the bondage of the actions. So should Arjuna act without any attachment. Control over senses and passions is essential to retain the discriminating power of the intellect.

Arjuna uvacha

Jyayasi chetkarmanaste mata buddhir janardana
tat kim karmani ghore mam niyojayasi keshava (1)

Arjuna asked— O Janardana, If you consider the path of understanding superior to the path of action, why do you involve me in this dreadful action ?

Vyamishreneva vakyena buddhim mohayaseeva me
tadekam vada nishchitya yena shreyo ahamapnuyam (2)

My intelligence is bewildered by your ambiguous words. Tell me definitely one thing by which I may attain the supreme.

Shribhagavan uvacha

Loke asmin dvividha nishtha pura prokta maya nagha
gyana yogena sankhyanam karmayogena yoginam (3)

Shri Bhagawan (Krishna) said- O Arjuna, I have always proposed two disciplines in the past, Sankhya-Yoga, the path of knowledge for those who meditate and Karma-Yoga, the path of action for those who believe in work.

Na karmanam anarambhan naishkarmyam purusho ashrute
na cha sanyasanadeva siddhim samadhi gachchati (4)

Without working one does not reach the state of being the non-doer, and by renunciation one does not achieve any knowledge.

Na hi kashchitakshanam api jatu tishthatyakarmakrat
karyate hyavash karma sarvah prakratijair gunaih (5)

At no time does man ever remain without working. One has to act out of the compulsions of natural tendencies.

Karme indriyani sanyamya ya aste manasa smaran
indriyarthan vimudhatma mithyacharah sa uchyate (6)

He who outwardly restrains his senses but keeps thinking about objects of sensation is a hypocrite.

Yasitva indriyani manasa niyamyarabhate arjuna
karmendriyaih karmayogam asaktah sa vishishyate (7)

But one who keeps the senses under control, and without involvement, uses the senses as faculties for action is a superior person.

Niyatam kuru karma tvam karma jyayo hya karmanah
sharirayatrapi cha te na prasidhyeda karmanah (8)

Action is better than inaction and sustenance of life is also not possible without work, so you must do your assigned work.

Yagyarthat karmano anyatra loko ayam karmabandhanah
tadartham karma kaunteya muktasangah samachara (9)

Man is bound by his actions and work done other than as a sacrifice is a bondage. As such you must act without attachment, like a sacrifice.

Sahayagyah prajah srashtva puro vacha prajapatih
anena prasavishya dhvamesha vo astvishtakamadhuk (10)

Lord Brahman created people with sacrifice and said that you will stand blessed with such sacrifice and sacrifice shall fulfill your desires.

Devan bhavayatanena te deva bhavayantu vah
parasparam bhavayantah shreyah paramavapsyatha (11)

Through this sacrifice you prosper the gods and the gods be gracious to you. Thus prospering each other without motives, you all attain the supreme good.

Ishtan bhogan hi vo deva dasyante yagyabhavitah
tair dattana pradayai bhyo yo bhunkte stena eva sah (12)

Satisfied by such sacrifices the gods will provide well for you. One who consumes such gifts all for himself without sacrifice (work) acts like a thief.

Yagya shishtashinah santo muchyante sarvakilbishaih
bhunjate te tvagham papa ye pachantyatma karanat (13)

Those who use what is left of the sacrifice attain deliverance but those who prepare/cook only for their own consumption incur sin.

Annad bhavanti bhutani parjanyad annasambhavah
yagyad bhavati parjanyo yagyah karmasamudbhavah (14)

Karma brahmodbhavam viddhi brahma
aksharasamudbhavam
tasmat sarvagatam brahma nityam yagye
pratishthitam (15)

Life originates out of food, food comes from rain, rain is because of sacrifice and sacrifice is born out of action. Action has inspiration of Vedas and Vedas originated from Brahma. As such the all pervading Brahma is always immanent in sacrifice.

Evam pravartitam chakram nanuvartayatiha yah
aghayur indriyaramo mogham partha sa jivati (16)

One who does not perform his duties in accordance with the world order lives sinfully and in vain.

Yastva atmaratir eva syad atmatraptashcha manavah
atmanyeva cha santushtas tasya karyam na vidyate (17)

But one who stays in his self, is content with his self and is satisfied within self has nothing left to do.

Naiva tasya kratenartho na krateneha kashchana
na chasya sarvabhuteshu kashchid
arthavyapashrayah (18)

Such a person has neither a cause (selfish motive) to work nor a reason to not work. He has no selfish interest in anything.

Tasmad asaktah satatam karyam karma samachara
asakto hyacharan karma param apnoti purushah (19)

As such you should keep doing your duty efficiently without any attachment, as this is the way to achieve the supreme.

Karmanaiva hi sansiddhimasthita janakadayah
lokasangrahamevapi sampashyankartumarhasi (20)

King Janaka and great men have found deliverance through detached action and so should you act for the sake of general good.

Yadyadacharati shreshthas tat tadevetaro janah
sa yat pramanam kurute lokas tadanu vartate (21)

Ordinary people always follow the conduct of, and the standards set by, great men.

Na me parthasti kartavyam trishu lokeshu kinchana
nanavaptam avaptavyam varta eva cha karmani (22)

O Arjuna ! I need nothing to do in the three worlds (heaven, earth, and the lower regions) and there is nothing desirable which is beyond me (I have nothing to gain out of My works) yet I am engaged in work.

Yadi hyaham na varteyam jatu karmany atandritah
mam vartmanu vartante manushyah partha
sarvashah (23)

O Arjuna ! This is because human beings follow me in every way and if I fail in My duty there may be ruin.

Utsideyurime loka na kuryam karma chedaham
sankarasya cha karta syamu pahanyamimah prajah (24)

If I stop My work life will be destroyed and I would be the cause of this disorder and cause for the destruction of the populace.

Saktah karmanya vidvanso yatha kurvanti bharata
kurya dvidvamstatha saktashchi kirshur
lokasangraham (25)

Just as the ignorant works out of sheer attachment, so zealously should the wise work, though without attachment, for the sake of the society, O Bharata.

Na buddhibhedam janayedagyanam karmasanginam
joshayet sarvakarmani vidvan yuktah samacharan (26)

The wise, who have elevated their self to the supreme, should not confuse the minds of the ignorant or lead them into inaction. Instead they should by their own conduct lead them to detached action.

Prakrateh kriyamanani gunaih karmani sarvashah
ahamkara vimudhatma kartahamiti manyate (27)

Actually all works are accomplished by the qualities of the nature. The ignorant, being deluded by their ego, feel they are the doer.

Tattvavittu mahabaho gunakarmavibhagayoh
guna guneshu vartanta iti matva na sajjate (28)

However, O strong Arjuna, the knowledgeable one knows the elements of traits and actions, and hence he is not swayed by them.

Prakrater gunasammudhah sajjante gunakarmasu
tan akratsnavido mandankratsnavinna vichalayet (29)

Those enamoured with the qualities of nature remain attached to their traits and works. The wise ones should not perplex these ignorant people.

Mayi sarvani karmani sanyasyadhyatmachetasa
nirashir nirmamo bhutva yudhyasva vigatajvarah (30)

Directing all actions towards omniscient Me, fight without desire attachment or remorse.

Ye me matamidam nityamanutishthanti manavah
shraddhavanto anasuyanto muchyante te
api karmabhih (31)

Those who always follow this principle of Mine, with devotion, and without fault finding, obtain liberation from the bondage of karma

Ye tvetad abhyasuyanto nanutishthanti me matam
sarvagyanavimudham stanviddhi nashtan achetasah (32)

But those who finding faults in Me do not follow this principle, consider them as ignorant, deluded and lost.

Sadrasham cheshtate svasyah prakrater gyanavanapi
prakritim yanti bhutani nigrahah kim karishyati (33)

Everyone follows the compulsions of his nature. The knowledgeable also endeavour according to their nature. What can insistence do about it ?

Indriyasye indriyasyarthe ragadveshau vyavasthitau
tayorna vashamagachchettau hyasya paripanthi nau (34)

Senses have their attractions and aversions. One should not come under their control because they obstruct the road to well being indeed, on one's path of self-realization.

Shreyan svadharmo vigunah paradharmatsvanushthitat
svadharme nidhanam shreyah paradharmo
bhayavahah (35)

Better one's own discernment, even if of lower value, than the law of someone else howsoever good. It is beneficial to die doing ones own duty and the law of other is fraught with fear.

Arjuna uvacha

Atha kena prayukto ayam papam charati purushah
anichchannapi varshneya baladiva niyojitah (36)

Arjuna asked- O Krishna ! If man commits crime in spite of himself, what impells him to act so ?

Shribhagavan uvacha

Kama esha krodha esha rajogunasamudbhavah
mahashano mahapapma viddhyenamiha vairinam (37)

Shri Krishna said-Understand anger, born out of passion (rajas) as avarice. It is wicked and an unsatiable enemy of man.

Dhumena vriyate vahniryatha darsho malena cha
yatha olbena vrato garbhastatha tene damavratam (38)

Just as smoke clouds the fire, dirt covers the mirror, and amnion obscures the embryo, so does passion cloud the intellect.

Avratam gyanametena gyananino nityavairina
kamarupena kaunteya dushpurena nalena cha (39)

O Arjuna ! This unsatiable fire of passion is the constant enemy of the knowledgeable as it engulfs the wisdom.

Indriyani mano buddirasya dhishthanamuchyate
etairvimohayatyesha gyanamavratya dehinam (40)

Residing in the senses, in the mind and in the intellect, this passion mesmerises the man by covering his wisdom, and deludes his soul.

Tasmattvam indriyanyadau niyamya bharat arshabha
papmanam prajahi hyenam gyanavigyan nashanam (41)

As such control these senses Arjuna and get rid of this passion which ruins the intellect.

Indriyani paranyahur indriyebhyah param manah
manasastu para buddhir yo buddheh paratastu sah (42)

Senses are superior to the body, mind is superior to senses, intellect is superior to mind, and what is subtler than the intellect is he (the self).

Evam buddheh param budhva
sanstabhya atmana matmana
jahi shatrum mahabaho kamarupam durasadam (43)

As such know your Self which is superior to even the intellect. Be firm O Arjuna, control the desires, and do away with this enemy passion.

CHAPTER IV

Krishna tells Arjuna, "I am unborn, imperishable, and establishing Myself in my own nature I come into being through My power , *maya* (illusion), for the cause of dharma (righteousness) in this world. Those who understand this and work without attachment come close to Me and attain My state of being. I am unaffected by my work for I have no yearning for the fruits of my actions. So does the wise man work, without attachment or dependence upon the results. Keeping self under control and being without desire the *yogi* performs actions through his body and its faculties, while he himself remains liberated from his own actions. So even as he does work he feels that he is not the one who is doing anything. Thus he is free of guilt and attains supreme peace and self contentment. You must also erase your doubts by wisdom and realize your own self."

Shribhagavan uvacha

Imam vivasvate yogam proktavan aham avyayam
vivasvan manave praha manur ikshvakave abravit (1)

Shri Krishna said-This traditional *yoga* was taught by Me to Vivasvan (sun-god) who conveyed it to Manu. Manu told about this to Ikshavaku.

Evam parampara praptam imam rajarshyo viduh
sa kaleneha mahata yogo nashtah paramtapa (2)

Thus handed over in succession from father to son, this karma-yoga was known to the ancient seers but with lapse of time, it was later lost in this world.

Sa evayam maya te adya yogah proktah puratanah
bhakto asi me sakha cheti rahasyam hyetad uttamam (3)

You are My friend and a devotee and so today I have revealed to you the same ancient mystery of the yoga which is so great.

Arjuna uvacha

Aparam bhavato janma param janma vivasvatah
katham etad vijaniyam tvamadau proktavaniti (4)

Arjuna said-You have been born later and sun-god was ancient born. How do I understand that you taught this yoga to sun-god at the time of creation ?

Shri bhagavana uvacha

Bahuni me vyatitani janmani tava cha arjuna
tanyaham veda sarvani na tvam vettha paramtapa (5)

Shri Krishna said-Both you and me have had taken several births. You do not know of them but I know, O Arjuna

Ajo api sann avyaya atma bhutanam ishvaro api san
prakritim svamadhisthaya sambhavamya atma mayaya (6)

Though birthless and imperishable, and being God of all people, yet I manifest by controlling my own nature form and come into being by my power of divine potency, *yogamaya.*

Yada yada hi dharmasya glanir bhavati bharata
abyutthanam adharmasya tadatmanam srajamyaham (7)

Paritranaya sadhunam vinashaya cha dushkritam
dharma sansthapana arthaya sambhavami yuge yuge (8)

O Arjuna ! Whenever righteousness is lost and evil rises I incarnate myself in every age and come into being for the protection of the good, for destruction of the evil, and for re-establishment of the righteousness.

Janma karma cha me divyamevam yo vetti tattvatah
tyaktva deham punarjanama naiti mameti so arjuna (9)

O Arjuna ! My birth and works are pure and divine, and one who knows me so is not reborn after leaving this body, but attains my state.

Vitaraga bhaya krodha manmaya mam upashritah
bahavo gyanatapasa puta madbhavamagatah (10)

Earlier also, getting rid of passion fear and anger, many of my devotees, purified by the penance of this wisdom, have already achieved My state of being.

Ye yatha mam prapadyante tanstathaiva bhajamyaham
mum vartmanu vartante manushyah partha sarvashah (11)

O Arjuna ! As men approach me so do I endow them. In their various ways people follow My path only.

Kangkshantah karmanam siddhim yajanta iha devatah
kshipram hi manushe loke siddhir bhavati karmaja (12)

In this world those who want fruits of their actions pray to the gods because in this world results of the actions are achieved soon.

Chaturvarnyam maya srishtam gunakarma vibh agashah
Tasya kartaramapi mam vidhya kartaramavyayam (13)

The four categories of peoples (namely the Brahman, the Ksatriya, the Vaisya and the Sudra) were classified by me according to their qualities and works. Though creator of this existence you should understand Me, the imperishable, as one who does not do anything.

Na mam karmani limpanti na me karmaphale spraha
iti mam yo abhijanati karmabhir na sa badhyate (14)

As I have no desire of the fruits of my works I am unaffected by my works. Those who understand Me so are never bound by the works.

Evam gyatva kritam karma purvair api mumukshubhih
kuru karmaiva tasmat tvam purvaih purvataram kritam (15)

In the past also the discerning seeking salvation performed their works so. So should you act as your ancestors did.

Kim karma kim akarmeti kavayo apyatra mohitah
tatte karma pravakshyami yajgyatva mokshyase ashubhat (16)

Even the intellectuals get confounded in discriminating between action and non-action. I shall explain you the essence of action so that you are delivered of the bondage of works.

Karmano hyapi boddhavyam boddhavyam cha vikarmanah
akarmanash cha boddhavyam gahana karmano gatih (17)

Profound are the ways of work. One must know what is work, what is malfunctioning (malfeasance) and what is non-acted performance of works.

Karmanya akarma yah pashyed akarmani cha karma yah
sabuddhiman manushyeshu sa yuktah
kratsnakarmakrit (18)

One who perceives action in inaction and inaction in action he is wise. Such a person is a yogi, who has performed all the actions.

Yasya sarve samarambhah kamasankalpa varjitah
gyan agni dagdha karmanam tam ahuh panditam
buddhah (19)

Whose righteous works are without motives and desires and whose actions are devoid of the ego of being the doer is the real intellectual.

Tyaktva karmafalasangam nityatrapto nirashrayah
karmanya abhipravratto api naiva kinchitakaroti sah (20)

He who gives up attachment to the works and to the fruits of the actions is free of worldly dependence. Content in his Self, even as he executes the actions he actually does nothing.

Nirashiryata chittatma tyakta sarva parigrahah
shariram kevalam karma kurvannapnoti kilbisham (21)

Keeping control over body, mind and the senses, having given up desires and objects of consumption, even as his body works he incurs no sin.

Yadrchchalabha santushto dvandvatito vimatsarah
samah siddhav asiddhau cha kritvapi na nibadhyate (22)

Content with what he gets, free of desires and envy, beyond the conflicts of joy and sorrow, even minded to success and failure, the *karma-yogi* is unaffected (bound) by the works he does.

Gatasangasya muktasya gyanavasthita chetasah
yagyayacharatah karma samagram praviliyate (23)

He who is free of attachment, pity and pride, and whose mind is steady in pursuit of wisdom, all his actions become inactions (get lost in the fire of sacrifice).

Brahmarapanam brahma havir
brahmagnau brahmana hutam
brahmaiva tena gantavyam brahma karma samadhina (24)

The offering is brahma, the sacrificial material is brahma, the fire is brahma, the devotee is brahma, and this action is also brahma. He who realises brahma in his actions, his fruit is also brahma. (He realises it as the system of brahma working on its own)

Daivam eva pare yagyam yoginah paryupasate
brahmagnav apare yagyam yagyenaivo pajuhvati (25)

Some yogis arrange to offer sacrifices to gods for worship while others sacrifice their self in the fire of brahma.

Shrotradini indriyanyanye samyamagnishu juhvati
shabdadin vishayananye indriyagnishu juhvati (26)

Some offer as sacrifice their hearing and other senses into the fire of self-discipline. Others offer sounds and other objects of the senses as sacrifice into the fires of the senses.

Sarvani indriya karmani pranakarmani cha pare
atmasamyama yogagnau juhvati gyanadipite (27)

Some sacrifice the works of the life force and senses in the profound fire of yoga in the shape of self-control, kindled by wisdom.

Dravya yagyas tapoyagya yogayagyasa tatha pare
svadhya yagyanayagyash cha yatayah
samshitavratah (28)

Some employ/offer (conduct/pursue sacrifice with) their material possessions, some their austerities and spiritual exercises while others their minds and learning.

Apane juhvati pranam prane apanam tathapare
pranapanagati ruddhva pranayamaparayanah (29)

Those yogis who are embarked in yogic practice reach the breathless state by offering inhalation into exhalation and vice versa as sacrifice.

Apare niyataharah pranan praneshu juhvati
sarve apyete yagyavido yagyakshapitakalmashah (30)

Other yogis regulate their diet and offer their inhalations as sacrifice into the inhalations. Through various and severe exercises/sacrifices the people get rid of their sins.

Yagyashishta amrata bhujo yanti brahma sanatanam
nayam loke astyayagyasya kuto anyah kurusattama (31)

O Arjuna, those who consume the knowledge that remains of the sacrifice attain the supreme. One who does not perform the act at all has no place of happiness on earth, how can it be in the other world.

Evam bahuvidha yagya vitata brahmano mukhe
karmajanavidhi tansarvanevam gyatva vimokshyase (32)

Many such forms of sacrifice are mentioned in the Vedas. All these sacrifices are born out of the actions of mind, senses and the body. Know them to be so and you will attain liberation from the bondage of works.

Shreyandravya mayad yagyajgyana yagyah paramtapa
sarvam karma akhilam partha gynane parisamapyate (33)

O Arjuna ! Pursuit through knowledge is better than pursuit by material sacrifice, for knowledge is the end (culmination) of all sacrifices.

Tad viddhi pranipatena pariprashnena sevaya
upadekshyanti te gyanam gyaninas tattva darshinah (34)

Learn from the philosophers this transcendental knowledge with humility and reverence. If you prostrate at their feet, render them service, and question them with an open and pure heart, the seers will guide you to knowledge.

Yaj gyatva na punar moham evam yasyasi pandava
yena bhutanyasheshena drakshyasy
atmany atho mayi (35)

With such knowledge you will be relieved of your confusions, and you will see all the beings/existences in yourself and in Me, O Arjuna.

Api chedasi papebhyah sarvebhyah papakrattamah
sarvam gynanaplavenaiva vrijinam santarishyasi (36)

Even if you be the most sinful, this wisdom like a raft shall deliver you out of the sins.

Yathaidhansi samiddho agnir bhasmasat kurute arujna
gyanagnih sarvakarmani bhasmasat kurute tatha (37)

As fire consumes the fuel so does wisdom consume (reduces the existence of) all the actions O Arjuna.

Na hi gyanena sadrasham pavitramiha vidyate
tatsvayam yogasansiddhah kalena atamani vindati (38)

In this world, there is nothing so sublime and pure as knowledge. He who has attained purity of heart through a prolonged practice of *karma-yoga* enjoys this knowledge in his Self on his own.

Shraddhavamallabhate gyanam tatparah sanyatendriyah
gyanam labdhva param shantim achirena dhigachchati (39)

Self restrained and diligent, the devoted man follows knowledge, and with knowledge attains divine peace.

Agyash cha shraddya dhanash cha sanshayatma vinashyati
nayam loko asti na paro na sukham sanshayatmanah (40)

Indiscriminate, sceptical and trustless people meet ruin. For them there is neither this world nor the next, nor any happiness for the people of who have doubts.

Yogasanyastakarmanam gyanasanchchinnasanshayam
atmavantam na karmani nibadhnanti dhananjaya (41)

O DhananjayA ! By *yoga*, he who dedicates all actions (to God) and by discrimination has cleared all doubts, such a self-controlled person is not bound by the works.

Tasmadagyana sambhutam hratstham gyanasinatmanah
chchittavainam sanshayam yogamatishthottishtha
bharata (42)

As such O Arjuna, get rid of your doubts caused by ignorance with the help of the power of discrimination. Be steadfast in the principles of the discipline of *yoga* (Self-knowledge) and prepare for the battle.

CHAPTER V

Krishna further explains that salvation does not lie in renunciation, but only in the unselfish performance of duties. Mere knowledge of this is not enough. It should reflect in one's actions also. The wise person, the *yogi,* remains in full control over himself and even as he is working, only his body and its faculties remain engaged (involved) in the work, while he perceives himself as liberated and doing nothing. Thus he attains internal peace. Devoid of the ego of being a doer he remains no longer attached to external objects. Understanding the transitory nature of external pain and pleasure the *yogi* treats them equally and seeks happiness within himself. Thus he attains the beautitude of God and rejoices through doing good to all.

Arjuna uvacha

Sanyasam karmanam krishna punar yogam cha shansasi
yachchreya etayorekam tanme bruhi sunishchitam (1)

Arjuna said-O Krishna, you praise reprieve from works as well as their unselfish performance. Which of the two is better for me ?

Shribhagavan uvacha

Sannyasah karmayogash cha nihashreyasakaravubhau
tayostu karma sanyasat karmayogo vishishyate (2)

Shri Krishna said-Karma sannyasa and Karma Yoga both are good. But unselfish performance (karma-yoga) of actions is better than renunciation of (release from) actions, being easier to follow.

Gyeyah sa nityasannyasi yo na dveshti na kangkshati
nirdvandvo hi mahabaho sukham bandhat
pramuchyate (3)

O Arjuna! He who has neither hate nor expectations, that karma-yogi is worthy of being considered an ascetic as he is blissfully free from the conflicts of the worldly bondages.

Sankhyayogau prathagbalah pravadanti na panditah
ekam apyasthitah samyagubhayor vindate phalam (4)

Ignorant people see action as different from renunciation (sacrifice). One who concentrates in either of them gets the same fruit of achieving the supreme.

Yat sankhyaih prapyate sthanam tadyogair api gamyate
ekam sankhyam cha yogam cha yah pashyati sa pashyati (5)

Salvation is achieved by men of wisdom as also by men of action. He who sees the two as same (ways of attaining the same consequence, i.e., deliverance) sees the truth.

Sannyasastu mahabaho duhkhamaptu mayogatah
yogayukto munir brahma nachirena adhigachchati (6)

But O Arjuna ! Renunciation without action is difficult. It is the devoted man of action who soon attains brahma.

Yogayukto vishuddhatma vijitatma jitendriyah
sarvabhutatmabhutatma kurvannapi na lipyate (7)

He who is in control of his mind and senses, who is pure and identifies himself in others, such a man of action is never affected by his works.

Naiva kinchit karomiti yukto manyeta tattvavit
pashyan shranavan sparshan jighrann ashnan gacchansvapan svasan (8)

Pralapan visrajan grihnann unmishan nimishann api
indriyani indriyartheshu vartanta iti dharayan (9)

The wise man, even as he sees, hears, touches, smells, eats, walks, sleeps, breathes, speaks, receives, gives, opens and closes the eyes, he feels that it is the organs (senses) which are engaged in their due natural activities, while he (Self) is not doing anything.

Brahmany adhaya karmani sangan tyaktva karoti yah
lipyate na sa papena padmapattramivambhasa (10)

One who, forsaking all attachments, submits all his actions to the supreme stays pure just as the lotus leaf remains untouched by water.

Kayena manasa buddhya kevalair indriyair api
yoginah karma kurvanti sangam tyaktva atmashuddhaye (11)

Discarding attachment to fruits of their work, these wise men put the body, the mind, the senses and the intellect into action, (as if only using them) for the purification of the self.

Yuktah karmaphalam tyaktva shantim apnoti naishthikim
ayuktah kamakarena phale sakto nibadhyate (12)

The wise (karma-yogi) finds divine peace in actions with no concern for the fruits of his actions, while the involved person, driven by the desires of the results, remains bonded.

Sarvakarmani manasa sanyasyaste sukham vashi
navadvare pure dehi naiva kurvanna karayan (13)

Having controlled his nature, the yogi dwells in the body as a pure self which neither acts nor gets actions done (remains aloof of the actions of the body).

Na kartritvam na karmani lokasya srijati prabhuh
na karmaphalasanyogam svabhavaastu pravartate (14)

God neither creates the acts, nor the cause, nor the circumstances of the actions (or their fruits). It is the nature which acts these out (nature takes its course of action).

Na datte kasyachit papam na chaiva sukrtam vibhuh
agyanena avratam gyanam tena muhyanti jantavah (15)

Even the omnipresent God does not accept acts of either sin nor piousness of men. The knowledge is obscured by ignorance, thereby men dredeluded.

Gyanena tu tada gyanam yesham nashitamatmanah
tesham aditya vajgyanam prakashyati tat param (16)

But for those whose ignorance is destroyed by the knowledge of supreme, those who know the ultimate reality see the supreme self clearly as if illuminated by the sun.

Tadbuddhayas tadatmanas tannishthas tatparayanah
gachchanty apunaravrattim gyananirdhutaklmashah (17)

Those who repose their entire being into (synthesise with) brahma are rid of the sins and achieve salvation.

Vidyavinayasampanne brahmane gavi hastini
shuni chaiva shvapake cha panditah samadarshinah (18)

These wise men see the same (brahma) in the knowledgeable and humble brahmin, the cow, the elephant, the dog and the pariah.

Ihaiva tairjitah sargo yesham samye sthitam manah
nirdosham hi samam brahma tasmad brahmani te sthitah (19)

Whose mind is firm in evenness of outlook (sees everything as same) wins this world in living state itself, because brahma is pure and is uniformly immanent in everything.

Na prahrashyeti priyam prapya nodvijet prapya cha priyam
sthirabuddhir asammudho brahmavid brahmani sthitah (20)

Who does not rejoice winning something pleasant nor regrets getting what is unpleasant, stable and unattached in mind, he stays steadfast in the *Brahma.*

Bahyasparsheshvasaktatma vindatyatmani yat sukham
sa brahmayogayuktatma sukham akshayam ashnute (21)

Detached from external issues (impulses), the seeker of the internal self attains the pure bliss of awakening. Thereupon transcending as the *Brahma* he attains eternal joy.

Ye hi sansaparshaja bhoga duhkhayonaya eva te
adyantavantah kaunteya na teshu ramate budhah (22)

Objects of (and hence the pleasures of) sensory contacts are exciting but they are shortlived and are causes of sorrow. As such Arjuna, the wise do not have any fixation for them.

Shaknoti haiva yah sodhum prak shariravimokshanat
kamakrodhodbhavam vegam sa yuktah sa sukhi narah (23)

He who can resist the impulses of lust and anger, he is the *yogi,* only he can be happy.

Yo antah sukho antararamas tathantar jyotir eva yah
sa yogi brahmanirvanam brahmabhuto adhigachchati (24)

He who is happy and content in self, who is wise within the self, he the knower of *sankhya-yoga* achieves harmony with *Brahma* and finds peace.

Labhante brahmanirvanamrashayah kshinakalmashah
chchinnadvaidha yatatmanah sarvabhutahite ratah (25)

He who is sinless, and whose confusions have been resolved by knowledge, who is occupied with (finds happiness in working for) the welfare of the people, whose heart is with the supreme, he achieves the serene brahma.

Kamakrodhaviyuktanam yatinam yatachetasam
abhito brahmanirvanam vartate viditatmanam (26)

For the calm and controlled sage who has realised the brahma, the ever peaceful supreme self is complete in all respects (end of all achievements, i.e., *nirvana*).

Sparshan kratva bahir bahyamsh cha
akshu chaivantare bhruvoh
pranapanau samau kritva nasabhyantara charinau (27)

Yatendriya manobuddhir munir mokshaparayanah
vigatechcha bhaya krodho yah sada mukta eva sah (28)

Unconcerned with external forces, coming out of the self, he who has controlled the senses, the mind and the intellect, is freed of desires, fears and anger, and is truly liberated at all times.

Bhoktaram yagyatapasam sarvalokamaheshvaram
suhradam sarvabhutanam gyatva mam
shantimrichchati (29)

He who understands Me as the end (culmination/ fruition) of all sacrifices, as God of all the gods, as an unselfish and sympathetic friend of all beings, finds peace.

CHAPTER VI

The detached person becomes a yogi and attains serenity by mentally uplifting (transcending) himself from his own limited beingness. All beings, everything, is the *Brahma,* and so realising the *yogi* sees everything as same (is even-minded in all situations). He is impartial to friends and foes and is same (even minded) to all sensations. His mind is at rest. He establishes a harmony with everything and treats everything/everyone equally, in the image of his own self. One is able to reach the state of a *yogi* by self-discipline, concentration and a life of moderation and control over senses. Mind is restless and difficult to control but it can be reined by constant practice. The yogi is better than the ascetic, the man of knowledge and the man of rituals. However those who are unable to attain this state of being a *yogi,* despite their inclination are also blessed because those who do good to others never face woe.

Shribhagavan uvacha

Anashritah karmaphalam karyam karma karoti yah
sa sannyasi cha yogi cha na niragnir na chakriyah (1)

Shri Krishna said-The person who does his rightful duties without depending on the fruits of his actions is the ascetec and the yogi. One who just abjures fire is not the ascetic and one who just abjures from the act is not a *yogi*.

Yam sannyasam iti prahur yogam tam viddhi pandava
na hyasannyastasankalpo yogi bhavati kashchana (2)

O Arjuna ! Understand *sanyas* (renunciation of the world) as yoga (discipline) as there can be no *yogi* who does not give up motives.

Arurukshor muner yogam karma karanam uchyate
yogarudhasya tasyaiva shamah karanam uchyate (3)

Work is the medium for salvation. Once the state of *yogi* is achieved and all motives have gone then peace is the means for knowledge.

Yada hi ney indriyartheshu na karma svanushajjate
sarva sankalpa sanyasi yoga rudha stadochyate (4)

When the person is attached neither to the sensory satiations nor to the motives of the acts, he is said to be a yogi.

Uddhared atmana atmanam na atmanamavasadayet
atmaiva hyatmano bandhur atmaiva ripur atmanah (5)

Bandhur atmatmanas tasya yenatmaivatmana jitah
anatmanastu shatrutve vartetatmaiva shatruvat (6)

For the one whose self has won over the control of the body and its faculties, the self is a friend. For one who does not have such control, the self is his own enemy. Man is thus his own friend as well as his own enemy and as such he should salvage, not imperil himself.

Jitatmanah prashantasya paramatma samahitah
shitoshna sukha duhkheshu tatha manapamanayoh (7)

The person with such an independent soul has only the supreme self pervading in his knowledge (mind) and so stays calm towards heat and cold, joy and sorrow, honour and disgrace.

Gyanavigyanatripta atma kutastho vijitendriyah
yukta ityuchyate yogi samaloshtashma kanachanah (8)

A *yogi* is internally surfeit with knowledge, is unaffected and self-controlled, and considers dust, stone and gold as the same. Such a yogi has achieved the supreme, so it is said.

Suhran mitra ary udasina madhyastha dveshya bandhusu
sadhushva api cha papeshu samabuddhir vishishyate (9)

He is even-minded (balanced/objective) towards friends enemies neutrals arbiters, haters, relatives, saints and the sinners.

Yogi yunjita satatam atmanam rahasi sthitah
ekaki yatachittatma nirashiraparigrahah (10)

Let the yogi control the body, including the mind and the senses, give up all attachments, and concentrate his internal self on the all pervading eternal supreme in solitude.

Shuchau deshe pratishthapya sthiramasanam atmanah
natyuchchritam natinicham chailajinakushottaram (11)

On clean ground, establishing his seat, neither too high or too low, spread on grass covered with clothes.

Tatraikagram manah kritva yatachittendriyakriyah
upavishyasane yunjyad yogam atma vishuddhaye (12)

Let him establish his seat in pure surroundings. There, controlling his mind and senses, let him practice yoga for self-purification.

Samam kayashirogrivam dharayannachalam sthirah
samprekshya nasikagram svam dishash cha
anavalokayan (13)

Prashantatma vigatabhir brahmacharivrate sthitah
manah sanyamya machchitto yukta asita matparah (14)

Erect and still, without allowing the eyes to wander, calm and fearless, let him be harmonized (intergrated) with Me.

Yunjann evam sadatmanam yogi niyatamanasah
shantim nirvanaparamam matsanstham adhigachchati (15)

The yogi who so concentrates on Me achieves the divine state of peace which prevails in Me.

Natyashnatastu yogo asti na chaikantamanashnatah
na chati swapnashilasya jagrato naiva cha arjuna (16)

Yukta ahara viharasya yukta cheshtasya karmasu
yukta svapnava bodhasya yogo bhavati duhkhaha (17)

Yoga is not by overeating or by fasting, not by sleeping or by being always awake. *Yoga* is being temperate (duly optimum) and moderate in conduct and actions .

Yada viniyatam chittamatmanyevavatishthate
nihsprahah sarvakamebhyo yukta ityuchyate tada (18)

When the mind is at peace, and so controlled that it gets stabled (integrated/harmonized with) in the supreme self, then the unattached person is said to have attained *yoga*.

Yatha dipo nivatastho nengate sopama smrita
yogino yatachittasya yunjato yogam atmanah (19)

The steadfast mind of the yogi is like a flame in a windless place, unflickering.

Yatroparamate chittam niruddham yogasevaya
yatra chaivatmanatmanam pashyannatmani tushyati (20)

Sukham atyantikam yat tad buddhi grahyam atindriyam
vetti yatra na chaivayam sthitash chalati tattvatah (21)

When the mind is at peace and integrated with the self, it recognises the self and is then content with it. The happiness which this gives cannot be grasped by the senses, but can only be felt by the mind. Such a stable minded and content person is never swayed from the truth (manifestations/forms) of the self.

Yam labdhva chaparam labham manyate nadhikam tatah
yasmin sthito na duhkhena guruna api vichalyate (22)

As he feels it (realisation of the divine in the self) to be the greatest gain, he desires nothing else and hence is never swayed by sadness.

Tam vidyad duhkhasanyoga- viyogam yogasangyitam
sa nischayena yoktavyo yogo anirvinnachetasa (23)

Yoga is this delinking from temporal grief. Practice it with perseverance, zeal and determination.

Samkalpa prabhavan kamamas tyaktva sarvanasheshatah
manasaivendriya gramam viniyamya samantatah (24)

Shanaih shanair uparamed buddhya dhritigrihitaya
atmasanstham manah kritva na kinchid api chintayet (25)

Giving up all cravings which arise out of desires, patiently controlling the senses with the mind, gradually place the mind in the supreme self and think of nothing else.

Yato yato nishcharati manash chanchalam asthiram
tatas tato niyamyaitad atmany eva vasham nayet (26)

Whatsoever ensnares this unstable and vulnerable mind, control and divert it back towards the self.

Prashantamanasam hyenam yoginam sukham uttamam
upaiti shanta rajasam brahma bhutam akalmasham (27)

For to the self realized yogi whose mind in perfectly serene who is free from sin, whose passion is subdued who is identified with supreme, the embodiment of Truth, knowledge and Bliss, supreme happiness comes as a matter of course.

Yunjann evam sadatmanam yogi vigatakalmashah
sukhena brahmasansaparsham atyantam sukham
ashrute (28)

The pious *yogi* by constantly integrating with his self experiences the divine pleasure.

Sarvabhutastham atmanam sarvabhutani cha atmani
ikshate yogayuktatma sarvatra samadarshanah (29)

With such *yoga* (integration) of evenness of mind, he sees the self abiding in all beings and all beings in the self . He thus sees everything the same.

Yo mam pashyati sarvatra sarvam cha mayi pashyati
tasyaham na pranashyami sa cha me na pranashyati (30)

He who sees Me (the universal self) abiding in all existences, and sees all existences in Me, he always sees Me and I always see him (he is close to Me).

Sarvabhutasthitam yo mam bhajatyeka tvam asthitah
sarvatha vartamano api sa yogi mayi vartate (31)

The *yogi* who, with evenness of mind, finds Me in all beings (everyone is the same Brahma) is always with Me.

Atmaupamyena sarvatra samam pashyati yo arjuna
sukham va yadi va duhkham sa yogi paramo matah (32)

O Arjuna, the *yogi* who sees all beings as same (sees others as equal with oneself) and finds joy and sorrow as same in all is the supreme *yogi*.

Arjuna uvacha

Yo ayam yogas tvaya proktah samyena madhusudana
etasyaham na pashyami chanchalatvat sthitim sthiram (33)

Chanchalam hi manah krishna pramathi balavad draiham
tasyaham nigraham manye vayoriva sudushkaram (34)

Arjuna said – O Madhusudana, the principle You have stated, of seeing everything same as oneself, this *yoga* (of evenness of mind) does not appear to be very sound to me. Mind is very fickle, impetuous and difficult to control, like it is difficult to stop the wind. So do I believe.

Shribhagavan uvacha

Asanshayam mahabaho mano durnigraham chalam
abhyasena tu kaunteya vairagyena cha grihyate (35)

Shri Bhagawan said-No doubt mind is restless and difficult to restrain, but it can be controlled with untiring efforts and by conscious detachment.

Asanyatatmana yogo dushprapa iti me matih
vashyatmana tu yatata shakyo avaptum upayatah (36)

I do believe that he who cannot control the mind cannot achieve *yoga* easily and one who endeavours to control himself can achieve it with effort.

Arjuna uvacha

Ayatih shraddhayo peto yogachchalitamanasah
aprapya yogasamsiddhim kam gatim krishna gachchati (37)

Arjuna said- O Krishna, what happens to one who has faith in *yoga* but being unable to restrain oneself, is unable to attain the pinnacle of the state of *yoga*.

Kachchinno bhayavibhrashtash chinnabhram iva nashyati
apratistho mahabaho vimudho brahmanah pathi (38)

O Krishna ! Ensnared in the path to achieve the supreme and without help, having lost both the pleesures, i.e., worldly and heavenly, like a scattered cloud, does the hapless person perish ?

Etan me sanshayam krishna chettum arhasyasheshatah
tvadanyah sanshayasyasya chetta na hyupapadyate (39)

O Krishna, only You are capable to clear such of my doubts, as I can find no one else.

Shribhagavan uvacha

Partha naiveha namutra vinashastasya vidyate
na hi kalyanakrit kashchida durgatim tata gachchati (40)

Shri Krishna said— O friend ! One who has lost his way so perishes neither here nor in the other world, for he who ever works towards general good never meets ill fate.

Prapya punyakritam lokanushitva shashvatih samah
shuchinam shrimatam gehe yogabhrashto abhijayate (41)

One who lost his way in *yoga* dwells in the world of the pure for years and then reappears (is reborn) in the home of the righteous.

Athava yoginam eva kule bhavati dhimatam
etaddhi durlabhataram loke janma yadidrisham (42)

Or else he may not go to the other world and may be born into a family of *yogi,* although such a birth is very rare.

Tatra tam buddhisanyogam labhate paurvadehikam
yatate cha tato bhuyah sansiddhau kurunandana (43)

Retaining his attainments of the knowledge of yoga from his previous birth, he thus resumes his quest for the supreme achievement with renewed fervour.

Purvabhyasena tenaiva hriyate hyavasho api sah
jigyasur api yogasya shabda brahma tivartate (44)

Compelled by the practices done earlier (in the previous birth) he is drawn towards yoga. Even he who does not wish to know more than what yoga is transcends (in achievement) what is described about brahma (in the Vedas).

Prayatnadyatamanastu yogi sanshuddha kilbishah
aneka janma sansiddhastato yati param gatim (45)

By practicing with effort (along with perfection achieved in previous lives), being pure and sinless, the yogi achieves the supreme state through good deeds.

Tapasvibhyo adhiko yogi gyanibhyoapi mato adhikah
karmibhyash chaadhiko yogi tasmadyogi bhava arjuna (46)

The *yogi* is superior to the ascetic scholar, superior to the knowledgeable person, and superior to one who works with the intention of personäl gains (results). As such, Arjuna you must become a *yogi*.

Yoginam api sarvesham madgatena antaratmana
shraddhavan bhajate yo mam sa me yuktatamo matah (47)

And of them all who are *yogi,* the one who with full faith totally offers (absorbs) himself into Me (fully integrates) is most superior and dear to Me.

CHAPTER VII

Krishna reveals his divine nature saying that it is very difficult to understand Him or His nature. He is the beginning and the end of the world. He is omnipotent, omniscient and omnipresent. He is the life in all existences and the existence itself has emanated out of Him, out of His resolve. Those who are led by their senses loose discretion and get carried away by illusions. People seek Him in distress, for knowledge and for wisdom. But those who are virtuous, devoted and seek refuge in Him transcend this skein of *maya* which He has created.

Shribhagavan uvacha

Mayyasaktamanah partha yogam yunjan maddashrayah
asanashayam samagram mam yatha gyasyasi
tachchranu (1)

Shri Krishna said – O Arjuna ! You shall know Me in completeness, through Me, by concentrating in Me, by practice of *yoga,* hear about it then.

Gyanam te aham savigyanam idam vakshyamy asheshatah
yajgyatva neha bhuyo anya gyatavyam avashishyate (2)

I shall reveal you in completeness the wisdom beyond which there remains nothing deserving to be known in this world.

Manushyanam sahastreshu kashchidyatati siddhaye
yatatam api siddhanam kashchinmam vetti tattvatah (3)

One out of thousands makes efforts to seek Me, and out of those striving yogins scarcely does one truly understand Me.

Bhumir apo analo vayuh kham mano buddhir eva cha
ahamkara itiyam me bhinna prakratirashtadha (4)

Apareyam itastvanyam prakritim viddhi me param
jivabhutam mahabaho yayedam dharyate jagat (5)

Earth, water, fire, air, ether, mind, intellect and ego these constitute nature eightfold divided. These are My lower (dormant/material) natures. My higher (active) nature is life force by which the world is kept in being (moving).

Etadyonini bhutani sarvanity upadharaya
aham kritsnasya jagatah prabhavah pralayas tatha (6)

O Arjuna ! Everything originates from these natures only, understand it so. And I am the origin and the dissolution of this world as well.

Mattah parataram nanyat kinchid asti dhananjaya
mayi sarvamidam protam sutre manigana iva (7)

O Dhananjaya ! There is nothing superior to Me and the universe is like a cluster of gems entwined (strung) with Me.

Raso aham apsu kaunteya prabhasmi shashi suryayoh
pranavah sarvavedeshu shabdah khe paurusham
nrishu (8)

O Kauntej ! I am the flavour in the waters, the candescence in the sun and the moon, the sacred word *(ohm)* in Vedas, the sound in the space and the manliness in men.

Punyo gandhah prithivyam cha tejash chasmi vibhavasau
jivanam sarvabhuteshu tapash chasmi tapasvishu (9)

I am pure fragrance in earth , the heat in the fire, the life in the living things and the effort in the ascetics.

Bijam mam sarvabhutanam viddhi partha sanatanam
buddhir buddhimatam asmi tejas tejasvinam aham (10)

O Partha ! Understand Me as the eternal seed of all existences. I am the intellect of the wise and the radiance of the radiant.

Balam balavatam chaham kamaragavivarjitam
dharmaviruddho bhuteshu kamo asmi bharatarshabha (11)

O foremost among the Bharatas ! I am the power of the unaffected. In beings I am the desire which is in accordance with righteousness.

Ye chaiva sattvika bhava rajasas tamasashca ye
matta eveti tanviddhi na tv aham teshu te mayi (12)

The tendencies of goodness *(sattva)*, passion *(rajas)* and darkness *(tamas)* all emanate from Me. But I do not abide in them nor do they (three) tendencies dwell in Me. (I am not controlled by them)

Tribhir gunamayair bhavair ebhih sarvam idam jagat
mohitam nabhijanati mamebhyah param avyayam (13)

Men get deluded with the activities of these three tendencies and do not see the eternal and unaffected Me beyond three modes of nature, i.e., Sattva, Rajas Tamas.

Daivi hy esha gunamayi mama maya duratyaya
mam eva ye prapadyante mayam etam taranti te (14)

This three faceted divine *maya* (creation) of Mine is difficult to fathom but those who concentrate on Me find their way of salvation out of this *maya*.

Na mam dushkritino mudhah prapadyante naradhamah
mayaya pahrita gyana asuram bhavam ashritah (15)

The dumb, the evil doers and those whose discretion is lost due to delusions/enticements do not follow Me.

Chaturvidha bhajante mam janah sukratino arjuna
arto jigyasur artharthi gyani cha bharatarshabha (16)

O Arjuna ! My devotees are of four types- the one in distress (the sad), the seeker of knowledge (the curious one), one who desires wealth (the worldly one) and the one who is wise (one who understands *Brahma* and wants to integrate self with *Brahma*).

Tesham gyani nityayukta ekabhaktir vishishyate
priyo hi gyanino atyartham aham sa cha mama priyah (17)

Of these, the wise and loving devotee is dear to Me, and as much as I am dear to him so dear is he to Me.

Udarah sarva evaite gyani tv atmaiva me matam
asthitah sa hi yuktatma mam evanuttamam gatim (18)

All the four types of devotees are blessed, I thus hold. But the wise is like Me as he has integrated himself with Me (resides in Me).

Bahunam janmanam ante gyanvan mam prapadyate
vasudevah sarvam iti sa mahatma sudurlabhah (19)

After several rebirths one gains the essential knowledge of elements. Everything is Me, rare is the sage who knows Me so.

Kamais tais tair hrita gyanah prapadyante anya devatah
tam tam niyamam asthaya prakritya niyatah svaya (20)

But those whose minds are led astray by desires, driven (compelled) by their own nature, they follow their own laws and worship their own gods.

Yo yo yam yam tanum bhaktah shraddhaya architum ichchati
tasya tasyachalam shraddham tam eva vidadhamyaham (21)

In whatever form the devotee intends to worship his god I strengthen his faith.

Sa taya shraddhaya yuktas tasya aradhanam ihate
labhate cha tatah kaman mayaiva vihitan hi tan (22)

Imbued with such faith he desires to worship his gods, and thence he also gains all he desires, though it is I who bestows it all.

Antavat tu phalam tesham tad bhavatay alpamedhasam
devan devayajo yanti madbhakta yanti mam api (23)

But their achievements are ephemeral. They attain the gods they worship, while My devotee, in whatever way he follows Me, attains Me surely at last.

Avyaktam vyaktimapannam manyante mamabuddhayah
param bhavam ajananto mamavyayam anuttamam (24)

The ignorant men, not aware of My indestructible and supreme state (beyond the reach of senses and mind), think of Me as subject to mortal things (merely as an apparent/physical expression).

Naham prakashah sarvasya yogamayasamavritah
mudho ayam nabhijanati loko mam ajam avyayam (25)

Veiled behind My divine potency *(yoga-maya)* I am not apparent to all. Hence these ignorant folk fail to recognize me, the unborn and eternal Supreme Deity.

Vedaham samatitani vartamanani cha arjuna
bhavishyani cha bhutani mam tu veda na kashchana (26)

O Arjuna ! I know all (beings) that is past, the present and to come, but there is none who knows Me.

Ichcha dvesha samutthena dvandvamohena bharata
sarvabhutani sammoham sarge yanti paramtapa (27)

O son of Bharata ! All beings, deluded by (suffering due to) the attractions of the joy and sorrow, which arise out of conflict of desires and envy, are subject to ignorance.

Yesham tv antagatam papam jananam punyakarmanam
te dvandva moha nirmukta bhajante mam dridha vratah (28)

But those who do good deeds without attachments and are steadfast in Me are liberated from such delusions. They only follow Me.

Jaramaranamokshya mam ashritya yatanti ye
te brahma tad viduh kritsnamadhyatmam karma chakhilam (29)

Those who under My refuge try to be free of death and pain, they have knowledge of the *Brahma,* of the absolute and of all the works.

Sadhibhutadhidaivam mam sadhiyagyam cha ye viduh
prayanakale api cha mam te vidur yuktachetasah (30)

Those who understand Me in My material and divine forms/aspects they know of Me and attain Me at last.

CHAPTER VIII

Krishna explains the concept of the indestructible, the *Bramha,* which is eternal, all pervading, ubiquitous and universal. Man emerges out of this indestructible, lives through a life span, and on death merges back into the indestructible. This cycle goes on and on. The yogi understands this phenomenon and through devotion to Him achieves salvation.

Arjuna uvacha

Kim tad brahma kim adhyatmam kim karma purushottama
adhibhutam cha kim proktam adhidaivam kim uchyate (1)

Arjuna asked-O supreme among men ! What is this Brahma ? What is knowledge about self ? What is action ? What is present in all beings and what is present in the gods ?

Adhiyagyah katham ko atra dehe asmina madhusudana
prayanakale cha katham gyeyo asi niyatatmabhih (2)

What is the part of sacrifice and how it is in the body ? How do the suitable minded know of You at their last hour ?

Shribhagavana uvacha

Aksharam brahma paraman svabhavo adhyatmam uchyate
bhuta bhavodbhavakaro visargah karmasangyitah (3)

Shri Bhagawan Krishna said-*Brahma* is the imperishable. The supreme essential nature (life form) is called the Self. *Karma* is the conduct (actions of sacrifices) which creates the beings (helps propagate/ continue the existence).

Adhibhutam ksharo bhavah purushash cha adhidaivatam
adhiyagyo aham eva atra dehe dehabhritam vara (4)

Whatever is subject to origin and destruction is the nature of being. The basis of divine is the pure spirit and basis of all sacrifices here in the body is Myself.

Antakale cha mam eva smaran muktva kalevaram
yah prayati sa madbhavam yati nasty atra sanshayah (5)

There is no doubt that one who departs from The body thinking of me alone even at his last moment, attains my abode.

Yam yam vapi smaran bhavam tyajatyante kalevaram
tam tam evai iti kaunteya sada tad bhava bhavitah (6)

O Kauntey ! Whatsoever a man thinks of at the last moment, he attains that, for he had always been absorbed by that thought.

Tasmat sarveshu kaleshu mam anusmara yudhya cha
mayyarpita manobuddhir mam evaishyasy asanashayam (7)

As such Arjuna ! Always keep Me in mind and fight the battle. So devoted to Me, you shall certainly attain Me if your mind and intellect are fixed on me.

Abhyasayogayuktena chetasa nanyagamina
paramam purusham divyam yati partha anuchintayan (8)

O Partha ! It is a law that he who practices constant concentration on the Supreme with an undeviating mind attains the Supreme.

Kavim puranam anushasitaram anor niyam ansamanu smaredyah
sarvasya dhataram achintyarupam adityavarnam tamasah parastat (9)

The person who thinks of the omniscient, omnipotent, most subtle, eternal, all sustaining, inconceivable, the self luminous like the sun, away from ignorance, pure and supreme.

Prayanakale manasa chalena bhaktya yukto yogabalena chaiva
bhruvor madhye pranam aveshya samyak sa tam param purusham upaiti divyam (10)

Having by the power of yoga firmly held the life breath in the space between the two eye-brows at the last time and then contemplating on the Supreme being with steadfast mind and devotion, he reaches verily that Purusha (God).

Yad aksharam vedavido vadanti vishanti yad yatayo vitaragah
yad ichchanto brahmacharyam charanti tat te padam sangrahena pravakshye (11)

Whom the scholars of Vedas call as imperishable, the state in which the detached ascetics enter, and the Supreme state for which people take vows, that Supreme state I shall describe for you now.

Sarvadvarani sanyamya mano hridi nirudhya cha
murdhny adhaya atmanah pranam asthito yogadharanam (12)

Om ity ekaksharam brahma vyaharam mam anusmaran
yah prayati tyajan deham sa yati paramam gatim (13)

At the last hour, one who controls all the senses, holds the life-force in the mind firmly, and concentrating in the Brahma pronounces ohm in His imperishable form, and thus thinking of Me, leaves the body, attains the supreme state.

Ananyachetah satatam yo mam smarati nityashah
tasyaham sulabhah partha nityayuktasya yoginah (14)

O Partha ! He who always thinks of Me and is always in harmony with Me easily reaches Me.

Mam upetya punarjanma duhkhalayam ashashvatam
napnuvanti mahatmanah sansiddhim paramam gatah (15)

Those who attain Me are not born again in this world of sadness and impermanence because they have attained the supreme perfection.

Abrahmabhuvanal lokah punaravartino arjuna
mam upetya tu kaunteya punarjanma na vidyate (16)

O Arjuna ! All worlds other than of Brahma are subject to (destruction) and reappearance/revival. One who attains Me is not reborn because I am beyond time while the worlds being bound by time are temporary.

Sahasra yuga paryantam ahar yad brahmano viduh
ratrim yugasahasrantam te ahoratravido janah (17)

Those who know that the day of Brahma losts one thousand Yugas (4.32 billion years) and that his night also lasts one thousand Yugas they know what day and night are.

Avyaktad vyaktyayah sarvah prabhavantya aharagame
ratryagame praliyante tatraiva vyaktasangyake (18)

Out of the non-apparent/unexpressed/non-being, all things emerge/find expression/come into being, with the dawn of the day of *Brahma,* and with night falling they all merge back (lose their expression) into the non- apparent *Brahma.*

Bhutagramah sa evayam bhutva bhutva praliyate
ratryagame avashah partha prabhavatyaharagame (19)

O Partha ! The very same existences, being in control of the force of nature, keep emerging at day and merging back at night (originating and perishing).

Parastasmattu bhavo anyo avyakto avayktat sanatanah
yah sa sarveshu bhuteshu nashyatsu na vinashyati (20)

Far beyond this unexpressed is the pure eternal wave which does never perish even after all existences have perished.

Avyakto akshara ity uktas amahuh paramam gatim
yam prapya na nivartante tad dhama par mam mama (21)

The state of non-expression (non-manifestation) is known as the imperishable. It is the Supreme state. Those who reach it do not return (or take rebirth). That is My supreme abode.

Purushah sa parah partha bhaktya labhyastva ananyaya
yasyantah sthani bhutani yena sarvam idam
tatam (22)

O Partha ! This supreme eternal purusha in whom all existences abide and who pervades in all existences can be attained only by singular devotion.

Yatra kale tvanavrittim avrittim chaiva yoginah
prayata yanti tam kalam vakshyami bharatarshabha (23)

O Bill of Bharatas ! I will now tell you how yogins departing from this world return or never return.

Agnir jyotirahah shuklah shanmasa uttarayanam
tatra prayata gachchanti brahma brahmavido janah (24)

There are two eternal paths, one of brightness and the other of darkness. One who follows the path of fire, light, brighter part of the month and the northern course of the sun attains the supreme.

Dhumo ratristatha krishna shanmasa dakshinayanam
tatra chandramasam jyotiryogi prapya nivartate (25)

One who is led through the path of smoke, night, dark half of the month and the southern course of the sun returns again.

Shuklakrishne gati hy ete jagatah shashvate mate
ekaya yatya anavrittim anyaya avartate punah (26)

In this world there are two traditional paths known, the brighter and the darker, one by which the person who departs achieves the supreme and the one by which the person who goes returns back to the cycle of birth and death.

Naite sriti partha janan yogi muhyati kashchana
tasmat sarveshu kaleshu yogayukto bhava arjuna (27)

O Partha ! Knowing both the paths the *yogi* is never deluded. So Arjuna always be equal minded and be firm in yoga (in My pursuit).

Vedeshu yagyeshu tapah su chaiva
daneshu yat punya phalam pradishtam
atyeti tat sarvamidam viditva
yogi param sthanam upaiti chadyam (28)

The *yogi* who understands this mystery in its elements transcends the achievements/attainments of (goes beyond the fruits of) study of Vedas, and other deeds of goodness. He attains the eternal supreme state.

CHAPTER IX

Krishna further elucidates the mystery of His divine nature telling Arjuna that although He is the source of this existence and sustains life but all beings do not dwell in Him nor does He abide in them. He keeps this cycle of rebirth going, sending people in this world according to His nature. He is everything as well as the process of everything but He is not bound or attached to this work He is doing. People have no control over this design of the system of His nature. Good deeds and pious conduct may bring them fruits of heaven, they may achieve knowledge about Him, but only absolute devotion (trust) to Him leads to salvation and brings lasting peace of mind.

Shribhagavan uvacha

Idam tu te guhyatamam pravakshyamy anasuyave
gyanam vigyanasahitam yajgyatva mokshyase
ashubhat (1)

Shri Krishna said-For the deliverance of an undoubting devotee as you, I shall repeat the knowledge of this secret science which is supreme and extremely pure.

Rajavidya rajaguhyam pavitram idam uttamam
pratyakshavagamam dharmyam susukham kartum
avyayam (2)

This is the supreme knowledge, eternal, most esoteric, pure and righteous. It delivers tangible results, and is easy to put into action.

Ashraddadhanah purusa dharmasyasya paramtapa
aprapya mam nivartante mrityu sansaravartmani (3)

O Arjuna ! Those who do not repose trust in it never attain Me, and forever wander in this world (remain mortal beings).

Maya tatam idam sarvam jagad avyakta murtina
matsthani sarvabhutani na chaham teshv avasthitah (4)

This universe is permeated by Me with My formless/non-expressed aspect. All beings are in Me but I am not in them.

Na cha matsthani bhutani pashya me yogam aishvaram
bhutabhran na cha bhutastho mamatma
bhutabhavanah (5)

And beings are also not in Me. Observe My divine yoga power that though it is My spirit which bears and sustains all beings, it does not abide in the beings.

Yatha kashasthito nityam vayuh sarvatrago mahan
tatha sarvani bhutani matsthani ityupadharaya (6)

Just as the air originating from the sky subsists in the sky so do the beings (who have originated form My thought) subsist in Me.

Sarvabhutani kaunteya prakritim yanti mamikam
kalpakshaye punas tani kalpadau visrijamyaham (7)

O Arjuna ! At the end of (a kalpa or a cycle of 4.32 billion years) all beings merge into My nature, and with the begining of the next Kalpa I recreate them.

Prakritim svam avashtabhya visrijami punah punah
bhuta gramam imam kritsnam avasham prakriter vashat (8)

Holding forth My nature, I keep creating this multitude of beings, enslaved by nature, again and again, according to their deeds.

Na cha mam tani karmani nibadhnanti dhananjaya
udasina vadasinam asaktam teshu karmasu (9)

O Dhananjya ! Those actions, however, do not bind Me as I stay unaffected and unattached to these works.

Mayadhyakshena prakritih suyate sacharacharam
hetunanena kaunteya jagad viparivartate (10)

O Kauntey ! Under My supervision nature creates the existences, and so does the world revolve.

Avajananti mam mudha manushim tanumashritam
param bhavam ajananto mama bhuta maheshvaram (11)

The ignorant, not understanding My nature, disregard Me as they find Me wandering in the human form.

Moghasha moghakarmano moghagyana vichetasah
rakshasimasurim chaiva prakritim mohinim shritah (12)

With their unstable minds, vain hopes, futile actions and ignorance, they adopt (are taken over by) the nature of deception and debasement.

Mahatmanas tu mam partha daivim prakritim ashritah
bhajanty ananyamanaso gyatva bhutadim avyayam (13)

But Partha ! great souls who have possessed by divine nature find in Me the eternal cause of existence, and knowing Me as imperishable follow Me with undistracted mind.

Satatam kirtayanto mam yatantash cha dridha vratah
namasyantash cha mam bhaktya nityayukta upasate (14)

These resolute devotees constantly chanting My praises, endeavour to achieve Me and engrossed in pursuit for My state of being, worship Me.

Gyanayagyena chapyanye yajanto mam upasate
ekatvena prithaktvena bahudha vishvatomukham (15)

Other wise persons even as they pray, they worship Me as the formless and unaffected Brahma. As one and yet as manifold, people worship Me in various ways.

Aham kraturaham yagyah svadhahamahamaushadham
mantroaham aham evajyamaham agnir aham hutam (16)

I am the rite, the sacrifice, the offering, the herb, the mantra, the ghee the fire and the oblation.

Pithamasya jagato mata dhata pitamahah
vedyam pavitram aumkara riksam yajur eva cha (17)

I am the sustainer of this universe its father, mother and grandfather. I am the object of knowledge, the purifier, the sacred syllaber OM, and the three vedas—Rig, Yajur, Sama.

Gatir bharta prabhuh sakshi nivasah sharanam suhrat
prabhavah pralayah sthanam nidhanam bijam
avyayam (18)

I am the supreme goal, supporter, lord, witness desirable abode, refuge, well-wisher, the origin and end, resting place, stare house the inherent seed.

Tapamyahamaham varsham nigrihnamy utsrijami cha
amritam chaiva mrityush cha sadasacchaham arjuna (19)

I emit the heat, and I regulate the rainfall. I am the death and I am also the deathlessness. I am being as well as non-being (what is and what is not).

Traividya mam somapah putapapa yagair ishtva
svargatim prarthayante
te punyam asadya surendralokam ashnanti divyan divi
devabhogan (20)

People who worship Me in accordance with the three Vedas, for the pleasures of the heaven, those pious people also attain the heaven as fruit of their good deeds.

Te tam bhuktva svargalokam vishalam kshine punye
martyalokam vishanti
evam trayidharmam anuprapanna gatagatam kamkama
labhante (21)

Having enjoyed heaven (consumed their good deeds for the pleasure of heaven) they return back to the mortal world.

Ananyash chintayanto mam ye janah paryupasate
tesham nityabhiyuktanam yogakshemam vahamy
aham (22)

To the devotees who are in meditation on Me and worship without desire, I provide for them means to achieve Me.

Ye apyanyadevata bhakta yajante shraddhayanvitah
te api mameva kaunteya yajanty avidhipurvakam (23)

O Kauntey ! Even those who trustingly worship other gods (for earthly gains) also worship Me only, but such worship if full of ignorance.

Aham hi sarva yagynanam bhokta cha prabhur eva cha
na tu mamabhijananti tattvenatashchyavanti te (24)

I am the recipient (consumer) and lord of all sacrifices, but those who do not know My true nature. So they fall (into the cycle of rebirths).

Yanti devavrata devanipitranyanti pitrivrattah
bhutani yanti bhutejya yanti maddyajino api mam (25)

People attain the gods they worship. Those who are devoted to Me attain Me. And so My devotees are never born again.

Patram pushpam phalam toyam yo me bhaktya
prayachchati
tad aham bhaktay upahritamashnami prayatatmanah (26)

With devotion whatever is offered to Me, be it a leaf, a flower, a fruit, or water, with love I accept it in material form.

Yat karoshi yad shnasi yaj juhoshi dadasi yat
yat tapasyasi kaunteya tat kurushva mad arpanam (27)

O Arjuna, whatever works you do, whatever you eat, whatever you sacrifice, whatever you donate, offer (devote) all of it to Me.

Shubhashubhaphalair evam mokshyase karmabandhanaih
sannyasa yoga yuktatma vimukto mam upaishyasi (28)

As such, with a mind so renounced, offering all works to Me, you will be released from the good and bad results (fruits) which are bound/linked with (are bondage of) works (actions) and thus you shall attain Me.

Samoaham sarvabhuteshu na me dveshyo asti na priyah
ye bhajanti tu mam bhaktya mayi te teshu chapyaham (29)

I have neither a friend nor an enemy and I pervade uniformly in all existences, but those who are devoted to Me are in Me, and I am in them.

Api chet suduracharo bhajate mam ananyabhak
sadhur eva sa mantavyah sanyagvyavasito hi sah (30)

Even if a sinner worships (follows) Me with devotion he should be considered a sage as his resolve is correct (righteous).

Kshipram bhavati dharmatma shashvachchantim nigachchati
kaunteya prati janihi na me bhaktah pranashyati (31)

He soon becomes a pious man and attains abiding peace. It is true Arjuna that My devotee never perishes.

Mam hi partha vyapashritya ye apisyuh papayonayah
striyo vaishyas tatha shudras te api yanti param gatim (32)

O Arjuna ! Whoever, be it women, traders, shudras and chandalas, howsoever base he may be, he attains the supreme state in My refuge.

Kim punar brahmanah punya bhakta rajarshayas tatha
anityam asukham lokam imam prapya bhajasva mam (33)

Then what to say of the pious men who attain the supreme state in My refuge. As such Arjuna, being born in a sad and temporal world always follow Me.

Manmana bhava madbhakto madyaji mam namaskuru
mam evaishyasi yuktvaivamatmanam matparayanah (34)

Fix your mind on me, be devoted to me, worship me and make obeisance to me, thus linking your self with me and entirely depending on me, you shall certainly realize me.

CHAPTER X

Krishna tells Arjuna that no one knows His origin because He is the source of origin. Everything, even all the feelings have emanated out of Him and there is no end to His divine manifestations. He is the Supreme Being.

Shri Bhagavan uvacha

Bhuya eva mahabaho shrinu me paramam vachah
yat teaham priyamanaya vakshyami hitakamyaya (1)

Shri Krishna said-O great warrior ! Yet again listen to My supreme words of secret wisdom as I love you and desire your welfare.

Na me viduh suraganah prabhavam na maharshyah
aham adir hi devanam maharshinam cha sarvasah (2)

Neither the sages nor the gods know of My origin for I am the premeval cause of (the origin) of the sages and the gods.

Yo mamalam anadim cha vetti lokamaheshvaram
asam mudhah sa martyeshu sarvapapaih pramuchyate (3)

He who understands Me as birthless (unborn) eternal and supreme God, such a wise person is freed of his sins.

Buddhirgyanamasammohah kshama satyam damah shamah
sukham dukham bhavo abhavo bhayam cha abhayameva cha (4)

ahimsa samata tushtistapo danam yasho ayashah
bhavanti bhava bhutanam matt eva prithagviadhah (5)

Intellect, knowledge, freedom from confusion, truth, restraint, poise, pleasure and pain, existence and non-existence, fear and fearlessness, non-violence, equanimity, contentment, austerity, charity, fame and infamy, such are the dispositions of beings. These diverse dispositions emanate out of Me only.

Maharshayah sapta purve chatvaro manavas tatha
madbhava manasa jata yesham loka emah prajah (6)

Etam vibhutim yogam cha mama yo vetti tattvatah
so avikampena yogena yujyate natra sanshayah (7)

All human generations have these dispositions having come up out of My resolve. One who knows in truth of this far flung power of Mine, is endowed with the pure knowledge of the yoga of devotion, there is no doubt about it.

Aham sarvasya prabhavo ma ah sarvam pravartate
eti matva bhajante mam budha bhavasamanvitah (8)

I, Vasudeva, am the cause of origin of the entire existence and the world moves because of Me. So knowing the wise worship Me with devotion and reverence.

Machchitta madgataprana bodhayantah parasparam
kathayantashcha mam nityam tushyanti cha ramyanti cha (9)

Constantly engaging themselves in Me, offering their lives to Me, enlightening themselves by conversing about Me, the devotees content in (rejoice in) following Me.

Tesham satata yuktanam bhajatam pritipurvakam
dadami buddhiyogam tam yena mam upayanti te (10)

Those who worship Me with such consistent devotion, I provide them with discipline of understanding by which they are able to reach Me.

Tesham evanukamparthamaham agyanjam tamah
nashyamy atma bhavastho gyanadipena bhasvata (11)

O Arjuna ! Out of compassion, I, as the flame of wisdom abiding in their souls, flare up Myself and remove the darkness of their ignorance

Arjuna uvacha

Param brahma param dhama pavitram paramam bhavan
purusham shashvatam divyam adidevamajam vibhum (12)

Ahustvamrishyah sarve devarishir naradas tatha
asito devalo vyasah svayam chaiva bravishi me (13)

Arjuna said-You are the supreme Brahma, the supreme abode, entirely pure, divine, eternal, the premeval god, unborn, and all pervading. All the sages have said so about you, and so please now You do tell me about Yourself.

Sarvametad ritham manye yan maam vadasi keshava
na hi te bhagavan vyaktim vidurdeva na danavah (14)

O Keshava ! I trust whatever You say. O Lord ! Neither the gods nor the demons know of your manifestation.

Svayam eva atamanatmanam vettha tvam purushottama
bhutabhavana bhutesha devadeva jagatpate (15)

O Creator of beings ! O God of existences ! O Lord of the universe ! O supreme soul ! Only You can know Yourself.

Vaktumarhasya sheshena divya hy atma vibhutayah
yabhir vibhutibhir lokan imamas vam vyapya tishthasi (16)

Only You have the capability to speak of Your divine powers by which You pervade the universe.

Katham vidyamaham yogimstvam sada parichintayan
keshu keshu cha bhaveshu chintyo asi bhagavan maya (17)

O God of yoga ! Always meditating upon You how should I know You ? And O Lord ! In what all forms do I deserve to think of You ?

Vistarenatmano yogam vibhutim cha janardana
bhuyah kathaya triptirhi shrinavato nasti me amritam (18)

O Janardana ! Relate to me again of Your yogic power and of Your manifestations for I still remain unsatisfied.

Shri Bhagavan uvacha

Hanta te kathayishyami divya hyatmavibhutayah
pradhanyatah kurushreshtha nastyanto vistarasya me (19)

Shri Krishna said -O foremost among the Kurus ! My divine forms are endless but I will tell you some of the prominent ones.

Aham atma gudakesha sarvabhutashya sthitah
aham adish cha madhyam cha bhutanam anta eva cha (20)

O Arjuna ! I am the soul (Self) established (seated) in all the beings. I am their beginning, their middle and their end.

Adityanam aham vishnur jyotisham ravir anshuman
marichirmarutam asmi nakshatranam ahm shashi (21)

Among the twelve sons of Adityas I am Vishnu, of the brightness I am the radiant sun, the power of the fortynine gods of wind, and moon among the stars.

Vedanam samavedo asmi devanam asmi vasavah
indriyanam manasha cha asmi bhutanam asmi cetana (22)

I am the *Sama-Veda* among the *Vedas* and *Indra* among the gods. Of the senses I am the mind, and of the existences (beings) I am the life force (consciousness).

Rudranam shankarash cha asmi vittesho yaksharakshasam
vasunam pavakshchasmi meruh shikharinamaham (23)

Of the eleven *Rudras* I am *Shankara,* of the *Yakshas* I am *Kuber,* the god of wealth. Of the eight *Vasus* I am *Agni* and *Sumeru* among the mountains with peaks.

Purodhasam cha mukhyam mam viddhi partha brihaspatim
senaninamaham skandah sarsam asmi sagarah (24)

Of the priests know Me as *Brihaspati*. O Partha ! Of the commanders I am *Skanda,* and ocean among the waters.

Maharashinam bhriguraham giramasmyekam aksharam
yagyanam japa yagyo asmi sthavaranam himalayah (25)

Of the sages I am *Bhrigu,* of the sounds I am the ***ohm,*** of the sacrifices I am the prayer, and among the stable I am the Himalayas.

Ashavatthah sarva vrikshanam devarshinam cha naradah
gandharvanam chitrarathah siddhanam kapilo munih (26)

I am fig among the trees, *Narada* among the seers, *Chitraratha* among the *Gandharvas* and *Kapila* among the sages.

Uchchaih shravasam ashvanam biddhi mam amritodbhavam
airavatam gajendranam naranam cha naradhipam (27)

Among horses know Me as *Uchchaihshravas, Airavata* among the elephants, and among humans consider Me as the King.

Ayudhanam aham vajram dhenunam asmi kamadhuk
prajanasha cha asmi kandarpah sarpanam asmi vasukih (28)

Of the arms I am the *Vajra,* of the cows I am *kamadhenu, Kamadeva* the premeval progenitor for birth of the child as per laws and *Vasuki* the king among the serpents.

Anantash cha asmi naganam varuno yadasamaham
pitrinam aryama cha asmi yamah sanyamatamaham (29)

I am *Sheshanag* among the nagas, *Varuna* the lord aquatic beings, *Aryama* among the pitras and also *Yamaraja,* the ruler.

Prahaladash cha asmi daityanam kalah kalayatam aham
mriganam cha mrigendro aham vainateyash cha pakshinam (30)

I am *Prahalad* amidst the demons. Of those who keep a count I am the Time. I am lion among the beasts and *Garuda* among the birds.

Pavanah pavatam asmi ramah shastrabhritam aham
jhashanam makarsha cha asmi srotasamasmi jahnavi (31)

Among the purifiers I am the air and of the warriors I am *Rama*. Crocodile among the fishes, I am *Ganga* among the rivers.

Sarganam adir antsh cha madhyam chaiva aham arjuna
adhyatmavidya vidyanam vadah pravadatam aham (32)

I am the beginning, the middle and the end of all existences. Of the learnings I am the science of knowledge of self. Among the debators I am the dialectic.

Aksharanamakaro asmi dwandvah samasikasya cha
aham evakshayah kalo dhataham vishvatomukhah (33)

Among the letters I am the first alphabet, (being the imperishable I am formless) and among the compounds (words) I am the constituent dualism. Timeless I am , I look on all sides and sustain the existence.

Mrityuh sarva harsh chaaham udbhavashcha bhavishyatam
kirtih shrivarak cha narinam smritirmedha dhritih kshama (34)

I am the destroyer death as well as the cause of all origin of future beings. Of the feminine traits, I am fame, prosperity, diction, memory, intellect, stability and forgiveness.

Brihatsama tatha samnam gayatri chandasam aham
masanam margashirshoahamritunam kusumakarah (35)

Of the hymns I am *Brihatsaman,* of *mantras* the *Gayatri,* of the months I am the first and spring among the seasons am I.

Dyutam chchalayatam asmi tejastej asvinamaham
jayo asmi vyavasayo asmi sattvam sattvavatamaham (36)

I am the gamble among the cheats and efficacy of the effective. I am victory of the winners, the industriousness of the resolute, and the purity of the pious.

Vrishninam vasudevo asmi pandavanam dhananjayah
muninamapyaham vyasah kavinamushana kavih (37)

I am Vasudeva among the Yadavas, Dhananjaya among the Pandavas, Vyas among the sages and Ushana (Sukracharya) among the poets.

Dando damayatam asmi nitir asmi jigishatam
maonam chaivasmi guhyanam gyanam
gyanvatamaham (38)

I am the rod of suppression, the strategy of victors. I am the silence of the secrecy and the wisdom of the wise.

Yachchapi sarvabhutanam bijam tada aham arjuna
na tadasti vina yatsyanmaya bhutam characharam (39)

O Arjuna ! I am the seed of all the existences, and there is nothing, moving or stationary, which is without Me (which can exist apart from Me).

Nanto asti mama divyanam vibhutinam paramtapa
esha tuddyeshatah prokto vibhutervistaro maya (40)

O Arjuna ! There is no end to My divine manifestations. What I have said must serve only as a brief example.

Yad yad vibhuti matsattvam shrimadurjitameva va
tat tadevavagachcha tvam mama tejo anshasambhavam (41)

All these divine manifestations that have vigour, energy and radiance, consider them as expressions of only a fragment of My power.

Athava bahunaitena kim gyatena tava arjuna
vishtabhyahmidam kritsnamekanshe sthito jagat (42)

But where is the purpose of knowing so much Arjuna ? I am holding this entire universe with only a fraction of My power of yoga.

CHAPTER XI

Arjuna expresses his keen desire to see Krishna in His divine form. To satiate Arjuna's curiosity Krishna bestows him with extrasensory vision and transforms Himself into *Viraat-roop* (divine form) while Arjuna watches Him stupefied. It is a shattering experience, a spectacle of radiance, a splendour of colours and dazzling lights in which Arjuna sees Krishna in infinite and terrifying forms. He also witnesses all men, his friends and enemies, stoically floating into the gigantic mouth of Krishna and being devoured in its raging fire. Krishna explains that even if Arjuna does not engage himself in the action of fighting in the battle (to avoid killing them) they would still all die. "I am time, and in fact all these warriors have already been slain by me." Krishna says Arjuna should not worry but fight and win glory and the kingdom.

Trembling with fear Arjuna prostrates before Krishna, acknowledges His might and begs Him to revert to His normal form. Krishna transforms back to His human form and says that His divine form cannot be seen by anyone in any way, but those who are devoted, who work in a detached way and are free of complexes towards others, can transcend and achieve the beautitude of god.

Arjuna uvacha

Madanugrahaya param guhyam adhyatma sangyitam
yattvayoktam vachas ena mohoayam vigto mama (1)

Arjuna said-My ignorance stands destroyed by the words of secret wisdom you have told me as a gracious favour.

Bhavapyayau hi bhutanam kshruto vistarsho maya
tvattah kamalpatraksha mahatmyamapi chavyayam (2)

Because O Lotus Eyed ! I heard of the origin and passing away of your existences, as well as of your imperishable splendour.

Evam etad yathattha tvam atmanam parameshvara
drashtumichchami te rupamaishvarm purushottama (3)

O Supreme God! As You say about yourself, it is so, but O foremost among men, I want to physically see your cosmic form, full of power, strenght, vigour, knowledge opulence and ardour.

Manyase yadi tachchkyam mya drashtumiti prabho
yogeshvara tato me tvam darshayatmanam avyayam (4)

O God ! If You consider that it is appropriate that I can see Your divine form , then O Lord of the yogis, do let me see your imperishable form.

Shri Bhagavan uvacha

Pashya me partha rupani shatasho atha sahasrashah
nanavidhani divyani nanavarnakrtini cha (5)

Shri Krishna said-O Partha ! Now you will see My hundreds and thousands of different and marvellous colours and forms.

Pashyaadityan vasun rudran ashvinau marutas tatha
bahuny adrishta purvani pashyash chaaryani bharata (6)

O Arjuna of Bharata clan ! Behold in Me the *Adityas,* the eight *Vasus,* the eleven *Rudras,* both the Asvins and the forty nine *Marutas*. Look Arjuna, for now you shall see wonders as never seen before.

Jhaian kashtham jagata kritsnam pashyadya sa characharam
mama dehe gudakesha yachchanyad drashtumichchasi (7)

O Arjuna ! Behold the entire existence, moving and non-moving , and whatever else you want to see, all at one place in My body.

Na tu mam shakyase drashtum anenaiva svachakshusha
divyam dadami te chakshuh pashya me yogamaishvaram (8)

But as you are not capable to see Me with these human eyes, I will provide you with divine vision with which you behold My divine creative power and glory.

Sanjaya uvacha-

Evamuktava tato rajanmahayogeshvaro harih
darshyamasa parthaya paramam roopamaishavaram (9)

Sanjaya said-O King! So saying the great Lord, destroyer of all sins, revealed His supreme divine form to Arjuna.

Aneka vaktra nayanam anekadbhuta darshanam
aneka divyabharanam divya anekoddyatayudham (10)

Divya malyambara dharam divya gandhanulepanam
sarva ashacharyamayam devam anantam
vishavatomukham (11)

With many mouths and eyes, with many sights of marvel, ornate with divine gems and arms, sporting garlands, clothes and aromas, made up of all wonders, endless and astonishing, with face turned to everyside, Arjuna saw the divine form of Krishna.

Divi surya sahasrasya bhaved utthita
yadi bhah sadrashi sa syad bhasas tasya mahatmanah (12)

Even if a thousand suns set ablaze together in the sky, it would scarcely match the radiance of Supreme Being.

Tatraikastham jagatikrtsnam pravibhaktam anekadha
apashyad deva devasya sharire pandavastada (13)

There Arjuna, son of Pandu, saw the whole world in the body of the God of gods, converged in one yet divided in multiplicity.

Tatah sa vismayavishto hrishtaroma dhananjayah
pranamya shirasa devam kritanjalirabhashata (14)

Thereafter, amazed and excited, Arjuna bowed down before the glowing God and spoke devotedly with hands folded.

Arjuna uvacha

Pashyami devans tava deva dehe sarvans
tatha bhuta vishesha sanghana
brahmanamisham kamalasanasth mamrishinshacha
sarvanugansha cha divyan (15)

Arjuna said-O Deva ! I see all the gods and many groups of beings in your body. I also see Brahma on the lotus throne, and the sages, and the divine serpents.

Aneka bahudara vaktranetram pashyami tvam sarvato
ananta rupam
nanatam na madhyam na punastavadim pashyami
vishveshvara vishvarupa (16)

O Lord of the universe ! With many arms, bellies, mouths and eyes, I see You from all sides in infinite forms. I do not see Your end, or Your center, or Your beginning.

Kiritinam gadinam chakrinam cha
tejorashmim sarvato diptimantam
pashyami tvam durnirikshiyam
samantad diptan larkddvitim prameyam (17)

I see You crowned, with mace and *chakra*, shining everywhere, dazzling the eyes with glory of fire and sun, incomparable and endless.

Tvam aksharam paramam veditavyam tvamasya
vishvasya param nidhanam
tvam avyayah shashvata dharma gopta sanatanastvam
purusho mato may (18)

You are the imperishable fundamental (to be known), the supreme refuge of the world, the eternal guardian of law (righteousness) and the primal purusha, so do I believe.

Anadi madhyantam ananta viryam ananta bahum
shashisurya netram
pashyami tvam diptahutashavaktram svatejasa
vishvamidam tapantam (19)

Without beginning, center or the end, with endless power and arms, with eyes like the sun and the moon, face with a fiery mouth, I see you blazing the world with your glow.

Dyavaprithivyor idm antaram hi vyaptam tvayaikena
dishash cha sarvah
drishtva adbhutam rupamugram tavedam lokatrayam
pravyathitam mahatman (20)

O Great soul ! The space between the earth and the sky is full of You, and the three worlds (Vishnu loka, Akshara Dhama/Parma Dhama) are agonized by Your divine and frenzied form.

Ami hi tvam surasangha vishanti kechid bhitah pranchjalyo
grananti
svastityuktva maharshi sidhasangha stuvanti tvam
stutibhih pushkalabhi (21)

Clusters of gods are entering into You, and some, terrified, pay salutations with folded hands, while the groups of sages saying 'blessed be' chant hymns in Your praise.

Rudraditya vasavo ye cha sadhya vishve ashvino marutash choshmapashcha
gandharvyakshasura siddha sangha vikshante tvam vismitasha chaiva sarvey (22)

The eleven *Rudras*, the twelve *Adityas*, the eight *Vasus*, ascetics, *Vishvadeva*, *Marutas*, *Gandharvas*, *Yakshas*, *Rakshasas* and groups of accomplished men, all gaze at You in bewilderment.

Rupam mahatte bahu vaktra netram mahabaho bahubahu rupadam
bahudaram bahundashtrakaralam drishtva lokah pravyathitas thathaham (23)

O Strong armed ! People are terrified at Your gigantic form, with several mouths, eyes, hands, legs, and teeth, and I am also afraid of it.

Nabhah sprasham diptam aneka varnam vyattananam diptam vishala netram
drishtva hi tvam pravyathita antaratma dhritim na vindami shamam cha vishno (24)

I find no peace at looking at You, glimmering and extended from sky to earth, with many hues, with mouth wide open and with large glowing eyes. My soul trembles at this sight.

Danshtrakaralani cha te mukhani drishtavaiva kalanala sanni bhani
disho na jane na labhe cha sharma prasid devesh jagannivasa (25)

I lose my bearings and peace as I look at your doom-like devastating devouring mouth, fierce due to molars. O God, have mercy on me.

Ami cha tvam dhritarashtrasya putrah sarvey sahevavanipalasanghaih
bheeshmo dronah sutaputras tathaso sahasmadiyair api yoddha mukhay (26)
vaktrani te tvaramana vishanti danshatrakaralani bhayanakani
kechidvilagna dasnantareshu sandrshyate churni tair uttamangaih (27)

All the sons of Dhritarashtra, and communities of kings are entering into You. Bheeshma, Drona, Karna, and all the main warriors of our side also are rushing inside Your mouth of fierce molars. Some are seen caught between the teeth, their heads crushed to powder.

Yatha nadinam bahavo ambuvegah samudramevabhi mukha dravanti
tatha tavami naraloka vira vishanti vaktranyabhi vijvalanti (28)

Just as rivers in their natural flow rush into the ocean so are the earthly warriors rushing into Your flaming mouth.

Yatha pradiptam jvalanam patanga vishanti nashaya samriddhavegah
tathaiva nashayavishanti lokas tavapi vaktrani samriddhavegah (29)

Just as moths, out of attraction, rush towards the blaze for their destruction so is everyone rushing towards Your mouth to perish.

Lelihyase grasamanah samantalokanmagran vadanair jvaladbhih
tejobhir apurya jagat samagram bhaasavograh pratapanti vishno (30)

Akhyahi me ko bhavanugrarupo namo astu te devavara prasida
vigyatum ichchami bhavantmaddyam na hi prajanami tava pravrittim (31)

Devouring the worlds from all sides, licking them repeatedly, O Vishnu, You scorch the whole universe with Your dreadful rays. Have mercy, I pray You. As I do not understand Your traits (way of working), Your having such a fierce form, do tell me who are You?

Shri Bhagavana uvacha

Kalo asmi lokakshayakritpravraddho lokansamahartumiha pravrittah
rite api tvam na bhavishyanti sarvey ye avasthitah pratyanikeshu yodhah (32)

Shri Krishna said-I am the Time, the wreaker of existences, risen (resolved) here to destroy the worlds. As such even if you do not fight, all the warriors set against you shall perish nevertheless.

Tasmattvamuttishtha yasho labhasya jitva shatrun
bhungashava rajyam samriddham
mayaivaite nihatah purvameva nimittamatram bhava
savyasachin (33)

All these warriors have already been slain by Me. You become only the executing/implementing cause (instrument). As such rise, defeat the enemies, gain glory and enjoy the prosperity of the kingdom.

Dronam cha bheeshmam cha jayadratham cha karnam tatha
anya api yodhaviran
maya hatams tvam jahi ma vyathishtha yudhyasva jetasi
rane sapatnan (34)

Do not fear. Kill the warriors Drona, Bheeshma, Jayadratha and Karna who have already been slain by Me. Undoubtedly you will win , so fight in the battle.

Sanjay uvacha

Etachchrutva vachanam keshavasya krit anjalir vepamanah
kiriti
namaskritva bhuya evaha krishnam sagadgadam
bhitabhitah pranamya (35)

Sanjaya said-Hearing so the words of Keshava, Arjuna, trembling and prostrating, with hands folded and voice faltering, spoke thus to Krishna.

Arjuna uvacha

Sthane rishikesha tava prakirtya jagat
prahashyatyanurjyate cha
rakshansi bhitani disho dravanti sarve namasyanti cha
siddhasanghah (36)

Arjuna said-O Omniscient ! People are rightly finding solace and delight in worshipping You. Demons, scared of You, are running in all directions, and the perfect ones are paying homage to You.

Kasmachch te na nameran mahatman gariyase brahmano apyadikartre
ananta devesha jagannivasa tvam aksharam sadasttatparam yat (37)

O Great Soul ! You are the supreme creator. Why obeisance be not paid to You, because O endless ! O God! Beyond what is apparent and what is inapparent, You are the imperishable *Brahma*.

Tvamadideva purushah puranastvamasya vishvasya param nidhanam
vettasi veddyam cha param cha dhama tvaya tatam vishvam anantarupa (38)

You are the first god, the primal purusha, the supreme abode/refuge, the knower and that which is to be known, the all present (existence being immanent with You), and infinite.

Vayuryamo agnir varunah shashankah prajapatistvam prapitamahashcha
namo namaste astu sahastrikratvah punashcha bhuyo api namo namaste (39)

You are the breeze, the Yama (death), the fire, the sea-god, the moon, and the premeval sacrificer (creator of eveything). I bow a thousand times to You. Again and again I greet You.

Namah purstadatha prishthtaste namo astu te sarvata eva sarva
ananta viryamita vikramastvam sarvam samapnoshi tato asi sarvah (40)

O most powerful ! I bow to You from front and from behind. I greet You from all sides, as You are everywhere. There is no end to Your prowess. Immanent in all, You are All.

Sakheti matva prasabham yaduktam hey krishna hey yadava hey sakheti
ajanata mahimanam tavedam maya pramadat pranayena vapi (41)

Yachcha vahasarthamast krito asi vihara shayyasana bhojaneshu
eko athava api achutya tatasamaksham tatkshamye tvamaham prameyam (42)

Forgive me for having at times been rash, even disrespectful, alone and in the company of friends. I have also used names loosely for You, calling You as O Krishna, O Yadava, O Friend, out of fondness and ignorance, as You are my friend. I was not aware of Your powers and such conduct of mine, unbecoming as it was, deserves to be pardoned.

Pitasi lokasya characharasya tvamasya pojyash cha gururgariyan
na tvatsamo astyabhyadhikah kuto anyo loka traye apya apratimaprabhava (43)

You are the Father of all the living and non-living existences of the world, the Supreme teacher and most respected, with unparalled power. There is no one equal to You in the three worlds, how can one be greater.

Tasmat pranamya pranidhaya kayam prasadaye tvamaham isham idyam
piteva putrasya sakheva sukhyuh priyah priyayarhasi deva sodhum (44)

As such O Lord ! I prostrate before You and pray that You may be happy. O Deva ! Just as father does to his son, a friend to his friend and a husband to his beloved wife, so You do pardon my faults.

Adrashtapurvam hrishito asmi drishtva bhayena cha pravyathitam mano me
tad eva me darshaya devarupam praseeda devesha jagannivasa (45)

Having seen this form of Yours not ever seen before, I am excited with pleasure as well as with fright, so please have mercy and come back to Your previous form. O Lord of the world, be pleased.

Kiritinam gadinam chakra hastam ichchami tvam drashtum aham tathaiva
tenaiva rupena chaturbhujena sahastrabaho bhava vishva murtey (46)

I want to see back wearing your crown with mace and chakra in Your hands.As such O God with hundred hands, please come back to Your normal form.

Shri Bhagavana uvacha

Maya prasannena tava arjunedam rupam param darshitam
atma yogat
tejomayam vishvamanantam adyam yan may tvadanyena
na drishtapoorvam (47)

Shri Krishna said-O Arjuna ! By grace and through divine power of *yoga*, I have shown you this extremely bright, primal and eternally infinite form of Mine which no one has ever seen before.

Na veda yagya adhyayanairna danairna cha kriyabhirna
tapobhirugraih
evamrupah shakya aham nriloke drishtum tvadanyena
kurupraveera (48)

O Arjuna ! In the mortal world I cannot be seen in this form either by study of Vedas, by knowledge of yajnas, or by exercises of charity (rites), or by rigours of austerity.

Ma te vyatha ma cha vimudha bhavo drishtva rupam
ghoram idringamamedam
vyapetabhih pritamanah punastvam tad eva me rupamidam
prapashya (49)

You should neither be frightened nor be bewildered by this terrifying form of Mine. With love, and free of fear, behold Me again at My earlier form bearing conch, chakra and mace.

Sanjaya uvacha

Ity arjunam vasudevas tathoktva svakam rupam
darshayamasa bhuyah
ashvasayamasa cha bhitam enam bhutva punah
saumyavapur mahatma (50)

Sanjaya said-So saying, Bhagawan Vasudeva reverted back to His normal form and consoled the terrified Arjuna.

Arjuna uvacha

Drishta vedam manusham rupam tava saumyam janardana
idanimasmi sanvrattah sachetah prakritim gatah (51)

Arjuna said ûO Janardan ! Now seeing You in this ever peaceful human form I feel stable and normal in my mind.

Shri Bhagavana uvacha

Sudurdarshamidam rupam drishtavanasi yanamama
deva apyasya rupasya nityam darshana kangikshinah (52)

Shri Krishna said-The divine form of Mine that you have seen Arjuna is very difficult (rare). Even the gods always aspire to see it.

Naham vedair na tapasa na danena na chejyaya
shakya evamvidho drashtum drashtavanasi mam yatha (53)

As you have seen Me, I cannot be seen so by Vedas, sacrifices, gifts or by rites of rigour.

Bhaktya tvaya anany shakya ahamevam vidho arjuna
gyatum drashtum cha tattvena praveshtum cha
paramtapa (54)

But O Arjuna ! By unfaltering devotion, My this form can be seen, understood and integrated (entered into) with.

Matkarma krinmat paramo madbhaktah sangavarjitah
nirvairah sarvabhuteshu yah sa mameti pandava (55)

O Arjuna, the one who performs all his actions for Me, is devoted to Me (considers Me as his goal), is without attachments, and free of ill-will towards all beings, such a steadfast devotee surely attains Me.

CHAPTER XII

Krishna tells Arjuna that those who are fully devoted are dear to him, but those who work in a detached way, as a *yogi,* truly get deliverance. This disposition can be attained by meditation, concentration , practice and through selfless actions. The true *yogi* is one who is free of ego and self sense, and bears no ill-will towards anyone. He remains even minded in pleasure and pain, is self controlled and self content, neither exudes nor receives commotion, detached and untroubled, of firm mind and determination.

Arjuna uvacha

Evam satatayukta ye bhaktastvam paryupasate
ye chapyaksharam avyaktam tesham ke yogavittamah (1)

Arjuna said-Between the devotee who is consistently engaged in worshipping You as a material being and the one who meditates upon You as the formless imperishable *Brahma,* who has the superior knowledge ?

Shri Bhagavan uvacha

Mayy aveshya mano ye mam nitya yukta upasate
shraddhaya parayopetaste may yuktatama matah (2)

Shri Krishna said-Those who concentrate on Me with single mindedness, and worship Me in material form, with trust and devotion, are very dear to Me among the *yogins.*

Ye tvanaksharam Nirdeshyam avyaktam paryupasate
sarvatra gamachintyam cha kootastham achalam dhruvam (3)

Sanniyamye indriyagramam sarvatra samabuddhayah
te prapnuvanti mam eva sarvabhuta hite ratah (4)

But those, who are ever equal minded, restrained, who worship Me as eternal, inexpressible, formless, omnipresent, inconceivable, impeccable, immovable and firm *Brahma,* and are engaged in the welfare of others with same feelings towards everyone, they certainly attain Me.

Klesho adhikataras tesham avyakta asaktachetasam
avyakta hi gatir duhkham dehavad bhiravapyate (5)

Efforts are tremendous for those who cling to the formless one, because the path of formlessness is attained by mortal beings with great pain. (It is difficult to pursue an abstract god without an assumed shape and character).

Ye tu sarvani karmani mayi sanyasya matparah
ananyenaiva yogena mam dhyayanta upasate (6)

But to those who place all their works in Me, are solely intent on Me, meditate upon Me, worship Me with devotion.

Teshamaham samuddharta mrityu sansara sagarat
bhavami nachirat partha mayyaveshita chetasam (7)

O Arjuna, I deliver those devotees out of the ocean of this mortal world, for their thoughts are always fixed on Me.

Mayyeva mana adhatsva mayi buddhim niveshaya
nivasishyasi mayyeva ata urdhavam na sanshayah (8)

Think about Me, apply your intellect in Me, then you will be with Me, undoubtedly.

Atha chitam samadhatum na shaknoshi mayi sthiram
abhyasa yogena tato mam ichchaptum dhananjaya (9)

If you fail to stabilise your mind in Me, then O Arjuna, try to reach Me by practice of concentration.

Abhyase apy asamartho asi mat karma paramo bhava
madarthamapi karmani kurvan siddhim avapsyasi (10)

If you are not able to do even such practice, then O Arjuna, you keep performing your works for My sake. By working as a service to Me you shall reach the same attainment.

Athaitadapy ashakto asi kartum madyogama ashritah
sarva karma fala tyagam tatah kuru yatatmavan (11)

If you are unable to do even this, then take refuge in devotion to Me, control your mind, and give up all the fruits of your actions.

Shreyo hi gyanam abhyasaj gyanad dhyanam vishishyate
dhyanat karma fala tyagastya agachchantir anantaram (12)

Knowledge is superior to practice of concentration, meditation is superior to knowledge, and renunciation of fruit of action is superior to meditation. Supreme peace is attained immediately/only after such sacrifice.

Adveshta sarvabhutanam maitrah karuna eva cha
nirmamo nirahankarah samaduhakh sukhahkshami (13)

Santushtah satatam yogi yatatma dridhanishchayah
mayyarpita manobuddhir yo madbhaktah sa me priyah (14)

The person who carries no ill-will towards anyone, is selfless, amicable, considerate to all without any motive, unaffected, ego-free, forgiving, equal minded in joy and woe, always content, self-controlled, resolute in Me, such a one who has established his mind and intellect in Me is dear to Me.

Yasmannodvijate loko lokanno dvijate cha yah
harshamarsha bhayo dvegair mukto yah sa cha me
priyah (15)

He from whom no one gets into commotion, nor does he get into commotion by others, free of joyous excitement (euphoria), fear, envy and agitation, such a devotee is also dear to Me.

Anapekshah shuchirdaksha udasino gatavyathah
sarvarambha parityagi yo madabhaktah sa me priyah (16)

The devotee who is without expectations, pure, intelligent, aloof (unbiased), free of sorrows, one who has no thought of (personal) genesis (in the work) is dear to Me.

Yo na hrishyati na dveshti na shochati na kangkshati
shubha ashubha parityagi bhaktimany sa me priyah (17)

He who never exults or hates, neither mourns nor desires, and has given up both the good and the evil, he is the devotee dear to Me.

Samah shatrau cha mitre cha tatha manapamanayoh
shitoshna sukha dukheshu samah sanga vivarjitah (18)

He who treats friends and foes, honour and dishonour, heat and cold, happiness and sadness alike, free of conflicts and is without attachments.

Tulya ninda stutir mauni santushto yena kenachit
aniketah sthira matir bhaktiman me priyo narah (19)

Who considers praise and criticism as same, is reticent and content with what he gets, not fixed with one dwelling place, whose mind is stable, he is the devotee dear to Me.

Ye tu dharmyamritmidam yathoktam paryupasate
shraddadhana matparama bhaktas teitiva may priyah (20)

Those devotees who repose their full faith in Me, and eagerly trust the immortal words of righteous wisdom I have just spoken are extremely dear to Me.

CHAPTER XIII

Knowledge is consistency, humility, integrity, patience, self-control, discipline steadfastness, purity and non-attachment. Real knowledge however is to know the *Brahma*, who is without a beginning, and said to be neither existent nor non-existent. *Brahma* is all pervading but too subtle to be known. Different people use different methods to understand this. He who realises His immanence, eternity and continuity, and the fact that his own life is ephemeral, attains the goal of wisdom. The wise man realises that all actions are done by the nature itself and so he is not the doer. The supreme self is immanent in the body, but it neither acts nor is affected by the individual's actions. Those who understand these distinctions attain the supreme state of peace.

Shri Bhagavana uvacha

Idam shariram kaunteya kshetram ity abhidhiyate
etad yo vetti tam prahuh kshetragya iti tadvidah (1)

Shri Krishna said-O Arjuna ! The body is known as the field, and one who knows this is the knower of the field.

Kshetragyam chapi mama viddhi sarvakshetreshu bharata
kshetra kshetragyor gyanam yat tay jnanam matam
mama (2)

The knowledge about the field and of the knower (about the *purusha* and the *prakrati*) is the truest knowledge. Know Me as the knower in all the beings, so do I believe.

Tat kshetram yachch yadrik ch yadvikari yatashcha yat
sa cha yo yata prabhavashcha tatsamasena me shranu (3)

How is this field, what are its characters, and why, and what are the affects of the knower, understand them briefly now.

Rishibhir bahudha geetam chando bhir vividhaih prithak
brahmasutra padaivashchaiva hetumad
bhirvinishchitaih (4)

This wisdom has been expressed by sages in many ways, and in several mantras and also in the Vedas.

Mahabhutany ahankaro buddhir avyaktam eva ca
indriyani dashaikam cha pancha chendriya
gocharah (5)

Ichcha dveshah sukham duhkham sanghatash chetana
dhritih
etat kshetram samasena savikaram udahritam (6)

In brief, the field (body) is said to be (made up of) along with defects/distortions. These are said to be the five fundamental elements, the feeling of being (selfness), the intellect, the unmanifested (the inherent nature/tendency), the ten senses, the mind, the five objects of senses (sound, touch, form/sight, flavour and aroma), and desire, hatred, pleasure, sorrow, the material aggregate of the body, consciousness, and patience.

Amanitvam adambhitvam hinsa kshantir arjavam
acharyopasanam shaucham sthairyam atma vinigrahah (7)

Humility, integrity, compunction, forbearance, simplicity, service of the teacher, purity, stability, and mental restrain.

Indriyartheshu vairagyam ahankara eva cha
janma mrityu jara vyadhi dukh dosha anudarshanam (8)

Indifference to all worldly pleasures, lack of pride, and frequent deliberation about the pains and blemishes of birth, death, old age and sickness.

Asaktir anabhish vangah putra dara grihadishu
nityam cha samachittatvam ish tanonishtopapattishu (9)

Lack of attachment to son, wife, home and money, and constant equal mindedness to all agreeable and dislikable occurrences.

Mayi chananyayogena bhaktir avyabhicharini
vivikta desha sevitvamartirjana sansadi (10)

Absolute discipline and constant devotion to Me, inclination for solitude and pure environment, and disinclination towards those who are engaged in worldly pleasures.

Adhatma gyana nityatvam tatva gyanartha darshanam
etaf jnanam iti proktam agyanam yadato anyatha (11)

Consistency in the knowledge of self and insight of divine in such pursuit, all this (qualities given in shlokas 7 to 11) is known as true knowledge. What is away from it is ignorance.

Gyeyam yat tat pravakshayami yanjgyatva amritamashnute
anadimatparam brahma na sattannasduchyate (12)

I shall now explain what is worth knowing, the wisdom which brings supreme bliss. This eternal Brahma is neither existent (matter) nor non-existent (non-matter).

Sarvatah panipadam tatsarvato akshi shiromukham
sarvatah shruti mal loke sarvam avritya tishthati (13)

As it bears all the dimensions, He has limbs in all the directions, and eyes, head, mouth, and ears on all the sides.

Sarvendriya gunabhasam sarvendriya vivarjitam
asaktam sarva bhrichchaiva nirgunam
gunabhokttra cha (14)

He bears the semblance of the senses, yet He is insentient. He sustains everyone, yet is unattached. Traitless (without any quality) yet He bears all the qualities.

Bahirantashcha bhutanam acharam charm eva cha
sukshmatvat tad avigyeyam doorastham
chantike cha tat (15)

He (*Brahma*) pervades inside and outside all that moves and that which does not move. He is also what moves and what does not. Being subtle/sublime, it cannot be known (by the senses). He is far and yet He is near.

Avibhaktam cha bhuteshu vibhaktamiva cha sthitam
bhutabhatri cha tajgyeyam grasishnu
prabha vishnu cha (16)

He is indivisible and yet seems to be spread among all beings. He sustains life as Vishnu, destroys as Rudra and recreates all the beings as Brahman.

Jyotisham api taj jyotistmasah param uchyate
gyanam gyeyam gyana gamyam hridi
sarvasya vishthitam (17)

He is the supreme ray of light, beyond all darkness. He is the knowledge, the object of knowledge, well established among us all.

Iti kshetram tatha gyanam gyeyam choktam samasatah
madbhakta etadvijnaya madbhavayop papadyate (18)

Thus has been briefly described as the field, the knowledge and the object of knowledge. Knowing the essense of this, My devotee attains My form.

Prakritim purusham chaiva viddhyanadi ubhavapi
vikaranshcha gunanshchaiva viddhi
prakriti sambhavan (19)

Know that prakrati (nature) and purusha (self/soul) both have always been there (they are beginningless), and know that qualities and traits/tendencies (along with defects and complexes) of all matter have their origin in nature (are creation of the nature).

Karya karana kartritve hetuh prakritir uchyate
purushah sukha dukhanam bhoktritve
hetur uchyate (20)

Nature is the cause of the effect, the instrument and agency (nature is the cause of the origin and the development of the body and its sensory appliances, and hence of their ways of functioning) while the self/soul is the cause of bearing (experiencing) of pleasures and pains.

Purushah prakritisthito hi bhungkte prakritijan gunan
karanam guna sanggo asya sadasdyoniajanmasu (21)

Being amidst (established in) nature, the self (purusha) bears the modes of nature, experiences its constituents out of attachments, which have been created by nature itself, and this association is the cause of the self/soul being born along with such traits.

Upadrashta anumanta cha bharta bhokta maheshvarah
paramatmeti chapyukto dehe asmin purushah parah (22)

Onlooker (detached witness), endorser (the supporter/conscience keeper), sustainer (of body and life), user (of the body), the purusha (self/soul) in ourselves is actually the Supreme.

Ya evam vetti purusham prakritim cha gunaih saha
sarvatha vartamano api na sa bhuyo abhijayate (23)

One who understands the self *(purusha)* and the nature *(prakrati)* along with their characteristics, attains salvation/reprieve even as he performs all types of works.

Dhyane natmani pashyanti kechidatmam atmana
anye sankhyena yogena karmayogena chapare (24)

Some look for the Supreme Self in self through self by meditation, some by the science of knowledge and subtle intellect, while the others by works (action).

Anye tv evamajanantah shrutvanyebhya upasate
te api chatitaranty eva mrityum shruti parayanah (25)

Those who have no such knowledge, but devote themselves (worship) out of what they have heard from others also achieve deliverance.

Yavatsanjayate kinchitasattvam sthavara janggamam
Kshetra kshetragya sanyogat tad
viddhi bharatarshabha (26)

O Arjuna ! Whatever beings originate, mobile and fixed, come into existence out of interaction of the field and the knower.

Samam sarveshu bhuteshu tishthantam parameshvaram
vinshyatsv avinshyantam yah pashyati sa pashyati (27)

One who sees the imperishable Supreme poised among the dying beings sees the truth.

Samam pashyan hi sarvatra samava sthitam ishvaram
na hinastyatmanatmanam tato
yati param gatim (28)

He who sees the Supreme everywhere, equal to everything, does no injury to his Self, and attains the supreme goal.

Prakrityaiva cha karmani kriyamanani sarvashah
yah pashyati tathatmanam akartaram sa pashyati (29)

And one who sees all actions being done by the nature, and the self as the non-doer sees the real truth.

Yada bhuta prithagbhavam ekastham anu pashyati
tata eva cha vistaram brahma sampaddyate tada (30)

The moment he sees the divergent aspects/ facets/forms of existences centred in the one Supreme, and all the existences expanding (emanating) out of Him, that is the moment of his attainment of the supreme state (he becomes *Brahma*).

Anaditvan nirgunatvat paramatmayam avyayah
sharirastho api kaunteya na karoti na lipyate (31)

O Arjuna ! Being beginningless and traitless, this imperishable Supreme Self, though being in the body actually neither acts nor is linked to (affected by) the acts.

Yatha sarva gatam saukshmyad akasham nopa lipyate
sarvatra vasthito dehe tathatma nopa lipyate (32)

Just as the air is not attached to anything , being subtle, so is the soul, though pervading in the body, is not attached to (affected by) anything done by the body, being without any quality/trait of its own.

Yatha prakashyatekah kritsnam lokamimam ravih
kshetram kshetri tatha kritsnam prakashyati bharata (33)

O Arjuna ! Just as one sun illumines the universe so does the knower (soul/self) lightens up the entire field (body).

Kshetra kshetragyayor vam antaram gyana chakshusha
bhuta prakriti moksham cha ye viduryanti te param (34)

Those who so understand the nuances between the field and the knower, and know of independence (deliverance of beings) from nature/*prakrati,* they attain the state of *Brahma.*

CHAPTER XIV

There are three constituents of nature, viz. *Satva,* i.e., goodness, *Rajas,* i.e., passion and *Tamas,* i.e., darkness. Either of these predominate in the individual. The *satvic* person is pure and pursues the path of knowledge to gain happiness. The *rajasic* person is ruled by his craving and greed. He is attached to his actions, which cause strife. The *tamasic* person is ignorant, indolent, negligent and lazy.

The person, who understands these constituents, and the nature itself as an agent, transcends all the three dispositions. He remains unperturbed and detached, knowing that the disposition is the agent, the instrument, which is performing the act.

Shri Bhagavan uvacha

Param bhuyah pravakshyami gyananam gyanam uttamam
yaj gyatva munayah sarve param siddhim ito gatah (1)

Shri Krishna said-I shall now repeat the most superior of knowledge by which the sages have found liberation and achieved the supreme state.

Idam gyanam upashritya mama sadharmyam agatah
sarge api no pajayante pralaye na vyathanti cha (2)

With this knowledge, having attained My state, people are neither reborn at creation nor do face pain at the end of the existences.

Mama yonir mahad brahma tasmin
garbham dadhamy aham
sambhavah sarva bhutanam tato bhavati bharat (3)

O Arjuna ! My fundamental nature as *Brahma* is the womb of all existences, and I bear all the beings in it by the coordination of living and non-living.

Sarva yonishu kaunteya murtayah sambhavanti yah
tasam brahma mahad yonir aham bijapradah pita (4)

O Arjuna ! The nature (prakrati) is like a mother that concieves for the birth of different bodies and I am the father that establishes the seed.

Sattvam rajas tama iti gunah prakriti sambhavah
nibadhnanti mahabaho dehe dehinamavyayam (5)

O Arjuna ! Satva, *rajas* and *tamas,* these three qualities are born of nature, and they bind the imperishable soul to the body.

Tatra sattvam nirmal atva prakashkamanamayam
sukhasangena badhnati gyanasangena cha nagha (6)

O siniess ! Satva being pure is without distortions and hence enlightens. It binds the soul/self to the body with wisdom and bliss.

Rajo ragatmakam viddhi trishna sanga samaudbhavam
tannibadhnati kaunteya karmasangena dehinam (7)

O Arjuna ! Rajas is born of desire and attachment. It binds the self with works and their results.

Tamastv gyanjam viddhi mohanam sarvadehinam
pramad alasya nidra bhistannibadhnati bharata (8)

O Arjuna ! The all alluring tamas is born out of ignorance. It binds the self to sloth, sleep and intoxication.

Satvam sukhe sanjayati rajah karmani bharata
gyanamabritya tu tamah pramade sanjayaty uta (9)

O Arjuna ! *Satva* directs towards happiness, *rajas* towards works and *tamas* covers intellect and directs towards indolence.

Rajasatamash cha abhibhuye satvam bhavati bharata
rajah satvam tamash cha eva tamah satvam rajas tatha (10)

O Arjuna ! overpowering Rajas and Tamas, Satva prevails overpowering Sattva and Tamas, Rajas prevails, even so, overpowering Sattva and Rajas, Tamas prevails.

Sarva dvareshu dehe asmin prakasha upajayate
gyanam yada tada vidyad vivraddham sattvam ity uta (11)

When wisdom (power of discrimination) rises in the body, mind and the senses, understand it as the rise of satva.

Lobhah pravrattir arambhah karmanam ashamah spriha
rajasyetani jayante vivrridhe bharatarshabh (12)

O Arjuna ! Greed, activity, beginning of selfish actions, unrest and lust, these grow with *rajas*.

Aprakasho apravrattish cha pramado moha eva cha
tamasyetani jayante viviriddhe kurunandana (13)

O Arjuna ! Ignorance, disinclination towards dutiful work, excitement, sleep and delusionionary tendencies are the signs of *tamas*.

Yada satve pravraidhe tu pralayam yati dehabhrat
tadottamavidam lokanmamalan pratipaddyate (14)

When one dies with satva in predominance, he attains to the highest pure heavens.

Rajasi pralayam gatva karma sangishu jayate
tatha pralinastam asi mudhāyonishu jayate (15)

Death with rajas in the ascendency leads to rebirth among those attached to action, while dying with tamas prevailing leads to birth in the wombs of the deluded.

Karmanah sukritusyahuh satvikam nirmalam falam
rajasas tu falam duhkham agyanam tamasah falam (16)

The fruit of piety (goodness) is satvic and pure, the fruit of *rajas* is sadness while the fruit of *tamas* is ignorance.

Sattvat sanjayate gyanam rajaso lobha eva cha
pramada mohau tamaso bhavato agyanameva cha (17)

Wisdom follows from Sattva and greed, no doubt from Rajas, likewise obstinate, error stupor, ignorance follow from Tamas.

Urdhvam gachchanti satvastha madhye tish thanti rajasah
jaghanya guna vrittistha adho gachchanti tamasah (18)

Those who are established in satva rise upwards, those in rajas remain in the center while those in tamas sink down.

Nanyam gunebhyah kartaram yada drashtanu pashyati
gunebhyash cha param vetti madbhavam so adhigachchati (19)

When one does not see the doer, but sees only these qualities (performing their acts), and also knows Me as behind these qualities, he truly attains My Being.

Gunanetanatitya trindehi deha samudbhavan
janma mrityu jara duhkhair vimukto amratm ashnute (20)

He crosses (transcends) the barriers of the three qualities of the body, and being liberated of birth, death, age, and all other sorrows, achieves the supreme bliss.

Arjuna uvacha

Kairlingai trin gunanetanatito bhavati prabho
kimacharah katham chaitams trin gunan atiartate (21)

Arjuna said-What are the signs of the person who transcends the three qualities, how does he conduct, and O God, how does he rise above these qualities ?

Shri Bhagavana uvacha

Prakasham cha pravrittim cha mohameva cha pandava
na dveshti sampravrittani na nivrittani kangkshati (22)

Shri Krishna said-He who neither despises enlightenment *(satva)*, activity/involvement *(rajas)* or delusions *(tamas)* when they arise nor longs for them when they cease.

Udasinavad asino gunairyo na vichalyate
guna vartanta ity eva yo avatishthati nengate (23)

Like a witness who remains indifferent/ unaffected by the provocations of the qualities, knowing that it is all the interaction of the qualities which is performing the works, he stands firm.

Samaduhkha sukhah svasthah
samaloshta shama kanchanah
tulya priyapriyo dhirastulya ninda atma sanstutih (24)

Always established in self, equal to joy and woe, having equal feelings towards dust and gold, knowledgeable, constant to agreeable and dislikable things, and bearing praise and blame with equal aplomb.

Manapamanayos tulyas tulyo mitra aripakshyoh
sarva arambha parityagi gunatitah sa uchayate (25)

Same in honour as in dishonour, without favours between friend and enemy, and free of ego of being the doer (initiator), such a person is considered as being above the qualities of nature.

Mam cha yo avyabhicharena bhakti yogena sevate
sa gunan sama tityaitan brahma bhuyaya kalpate (26)

He who stays firmly devoted to Me also transcends the three qualities and achieves the state of Brahma.

Brahmano hi pratishthaham amratasya vyavasya cha
shashvatasya cha dharmasya sukhasyai kantikasya cha (27)

For I am the home of the eternal imperishable brahma, of the established law, and of indivisible bliss.

CHAPTER XV

In the first part of this chapter Shri Krishna describes about the structure of the world with an analogy of the *peepal* (fig) tree. This tree is having its roots from above (in the creator) and the branches, i.e., its manifestations below. As with the tree, the world wraps the human being among its branches, roots and leaves. It is necessary to understand this tree. The tree is not what it seems to be. The real form of this tree is not visible/discernable by means of tactile measurements, nor can it be understood by sensory perceptions. Its material form is beyond the measurable dimensions of time and space, being dynamic and eternal. Our sensory perceptions also are affected by the qualities of nature, thus vitiating our perception . We are taken over by the facade of its appearances, and we get entangled in the skein (roots and branches) of complexities, making the fig tree difficult to understand.

This understanding can be achieved only by removing the facade of apparent things, by cutting down our own notions, by literally going to the roots of the subject, by being objective in our perception in a holistic way. We should be able to see things without the bias of the selfness. This is described as cutting of the tree with the axe of detachment. It is a sort of ruthless introspection for the sake of better perspective.

In the second part of the chapter Shri Krishna also tells about His omnipotence and about His all pervading nature, and about His being the supreme person.

Shri Bhagavana uvacha

Urdhvamulam adhahshakham asvattham prahur avyayam
chchandamsi yasya parnani yastam veda sa vedavit (1)

Shri Krishna said—This world-form (fig) tree, the root of which is the primal purusha, and form of brahma is the main shoot, the leaves of which are the Vedas, he who understands about its leaves and the branches has true knowledge.

Adhashchordhvam prasritas tasya shakha guna pravrddha vishaya pravalah
adhsh cha mulanyanu santatani karmanu bandhini manushya loke (2)

The branches of this tree are nourished by the water of the three qualities. They extend and are spread everywhere. These branches have leaves in form of objects of senses (eg. see, smell, hear, taste, or feel). So stretch forth its roots, binding everyone according to the works.

Na rupamasyeha tathopa labhyate nanto na chadirna cha sampratishtha
asvattham enam suvirudhamoolam asanga shastrena dradhena chchitva (3)

The tree is not as it appears to be. This tree has neither a starting point nor any end point. It even has no established (firm) location. The tree needs to be cut.

Tatah padam tat parimargitavyam yasmin gata na nivartanti bhuyah
tameva chadyam purusham prapaddye yatah pravrittih prasrata purani (4)

After that, one should search for the supreme place (home) from where it is impossible to return back. There one should feel being in the shelter of the primal *purusha* from which the entire existence has spread. So should one be devoted to Him.

Nirmana moha jitasangadosha adhyatmanitya vinivrittakamah
dvandvair vimuktah sukha dukha sangair gachchanty amudhah padam avyayam tat (5)

Those who have lost attachment and pride, who have overcome cravings, who have no more desires, and are free of the dualities of joy and woe, such wise people achieve the supreme place (home).

Na tad bhasyate suryo na shashanko na pavakah
yadgatva na nivartante taddhama paramam mama (6)

The supreme home, from where no one returns, can be illuminated neither by the sun nor by the moon, nor by fire. It is self-luminous, being My abode.

Mamaivansho jivaloke jivabhutah sanatanah
manah shashthani indriyani prakritisthani karshati (7)

The soul/self in the body is My part only, and when in the state of nature (when in the embodied form) it attracts the mind and the senses.

Shariram yadvapnoti yachchapyutkramatishvarch
grihitvaitani sanyati vayur gandhan ivashayat (8)

As the winds carry the fragrance, so carries the soul, absorbing the mind and senses of the discarded body, to the next body.

Shrotram chakshuh sparshanam cha rasanam
ghranam eva cha
adhishthaya manashchayam vishayanupasevate (9)

The self enjoys the objects of senses through the organs of the body only, by ruling over it.

Utkramantam sthitam vapi bhunjanam va gunavintam
vimudha nanupashyanti pashyanti gyana chakshusah (10)

The ignorant (the deluded ones) do not realise/ see this (indwelling) self even as it stays, enjoys, experiences and departs from the body. Only the wise and discreet are able to know about it.

Yatanto yoginsha chainam pashyantyatmany avasthitam
yatanto apya akritatmano nainam pashyantya
achetasah (11)

Making efforts the yogins see this soul (self) in themselves, but those who are not internally pure, such ignorant people cannot see it even if they make efforts.

Yadaditya gatam tejo jagadbhasyate akhilam
yachchandramasi yachchagnau tattejo viddhi
mamakam (12)

Understand the radiance of the sun, which illuminates the world, and the radiance of the moon, and of the fire is My radiance.

Gamavishya cha bhutani dharayamy aham ojasa
pushnami chaushadih sarvah somo bhutva rasatmakah (13)

Entering the world I bear all the beings with My power, and becoming moon, the sap of life, I cause all the herbs to foster.

Aham vaishvanaro bhutva praninam deham ashritah
pranapana samayuktah pachamy
annam chaturvidham (14)

I am the digestive fire in the body , conjoined with the inward and outward breaths, I am the life force in all living beings.

Sarvasya chaham hridi sanvishtho mattah smritir gyanam
apohanam cha
veedaish cha sarvairaham eva vedy vedantakrid
vedavideva chaham (15)

I am in all the beings, omniscient, source of memory, knowledge and reason. I am what is to be known in the Vedas. I am the author and the knower of the Vedas as well.

Dvav imau purushau loke ksharash cha akshara eva cha
ksharah sarvani bhutani kootastho akshara uchyate (16)

There are perishable and imperishable existences in this world. The body is the perishable while the inapparent/hidden is the imperishable.

Uttamah purushas tv anyah paramatmetyu udahritah
yo lokatrayam avishaya bibharty avyava ishvarah (17)

But superior even to these two is different, the highest, the Supreme Self, as the eternal god, He enters the three worlds and sustains them.

Yasmat atksharam akito aham sharadi api chottamah
ato asmi loke vede cha prathitah purushottamah (18)

Since I transcend the perishable, and I am more exalted than the eternal self also, I am extolled as the Supreme Person in the Vedas and in the worlds.

Yo mam evam asammudho janati purushottamam
sa sarvavid bhajati mam sarva bhavena bharata (19)

O Arjuna, Those who know Me and accept Me as the Supreme person know all, and worship Me wholeheartedly.

Iti guhyatamam shastram idam uktam mayanagha
etad buddhava buddh uman syat kritakrityashcha
bharata (20)

O Arjuna, so has the most esoteric knowledge been imparted to you by Me. Knowing this man becomes wise and achieves fulfillment.

CHAPTER XVI

Shri Krishna tells Arjuna the characteristics of the divine properties as distinct from the properties of demoniac people. The individuals with divine nature have traits like fearlessness, purity of mind, self-control, uprightness, truthfulness, aversion to faultfinding, compassion to living beings, modesty, forgiveness, vigour, tranquillity, concentration, freedom from malice, covetousness and pride. On the other hand, traits of those with demoniac properties are ostentation, arrogance, vanity, harshness, ignorance, cruelty, proneness to anger, obsession with desires, conceit, obstination and total self-centeredness. There is no salvation for those with demoniac traits.

Shri Bhagavana uvacha

Abhayam sattvasamshuddhir gyanyoga vyavasthitih
danam damash ch yaghsh ch svaadhyayas tapa
arjavam (1)

Shri Krishna said-Absence of fear, inner purity, stability in meditation, resolution of knowledge, charity, restrain, reverence, righteous conduct, study of the Vedas, diligence and success.

Ahinsa satyam akrodhastyagah shantir apaishunam
daya bhuteshav aloluptvam mardavam hrir achapalam (2)

Non-violence, truth, calm, sacrifice, love for peace, absence of back biting, sympathy, freedom from greed, humility, bashfulness and poise.

Tejah kshama dhritih shaucham adroho nati manita
bhavanti sampadam daivim abhijatasya bharata (3)

O Arjuna, Radiance, forgiveness, patience, non-hatred, and moderation, these are the signs of people who are born with divine virtuls.

Dambho darpo abhiman cha krodhah parushyam eva cha
agyanam cha bhijatasya partha sampadam asurim (4)

Hypocrisy, pride, conceit, anger, foul-mouthedness, and ignorance, these are the marks of those people who are born with devilish properties, O Arjuna.

Daivi sampad vimokshaya nibandhaya suri mata
ma shuchah sampadam daivim abhijato sipandava (5)

Divine traits are conducive for attaining salvation/liberation while demoniac property leads to bondage. You should not get worried Arjuna as you are born with divine properties.

Dvau bhutasargau loke smin daiva asura eva cha
daivo vistarashah prokta asuram partha me shranu (6)

People are of two types only, those with divine nature and the others with devilish nature. As the divine property has already been elaborated, listen now about the demoniac property, O Arjuna.

Pravrittim cha nivrittim cha jana na vidur asurah
na shaucham napi cha charo na satyam teshu vidyate (7)

Demoniac people are not conscious either of the beginning of creative action nor of cessation/conclusion/renunciation of action. They are impure, untruthful and poor in conduct and in morality.

Asatyam apraihishtam te jagad ahur anishvaram
aparasparasambhutam kim anyat kamahaitukam (8)

They consider existence as unreal (superficial), without a foundation, and without a god. They think that the world has come up only out of the union of male with the female, and as such procreation/lust/desire is the only cause of existence, and that there is no other reason of existence.

Etam drishtim avashtabhya nashtatmano lpabhuddhayah
prabhavanty ugrakarmanah kshayaya jagato hitah (9)

Holding on to this falsehood, these people, whose nature is destroyed (who have lost sense of their self), and mind is dull, insulting and cruel to all, they stand up as enemy of the humanity only for its destruction.

Kamam ashritya dushpuram dambhamanama danvitah
mohad grihitva sadgrahan pravartante shuchivratah (10)

Vain, arrogant, hypocritical, deluded by pride, accepting false doctrines, they are ready to indulge into any type of sinful activity to fulfill their impossible resolutions, and lead a life of depravity.

Chintam aparimeyam cha pralayantam upashritah
kamopabhogaparama etavad iti nishchitah (11)

Obsessed with endless worries till death, engaged to the objects of satiation, they feel only this is pleasure.

Ashapashashatair baddhah kamakrodhaparayanah
ihante kamabhogartham anyayena rathsamcahyan (12)

Given to lust and anger, and bound by expectations, they are always making efforts to amass wealth by unfair means for the enjoyment of their sensuous pleasures.

Edam adya maya labdham imam prapsye manoratham
idam asti dam api me bhavishyati punar dhanam (13)

They are only thinking about what they have gained today, what desire they have fulfilled and what wealth they have to gain.

Asau maya hatah shatrur hanishye cha paran api
ishvaro ham aham bhogi siddhoaham balavan sukhi (14)

They are concerned about the enemies they have hit and the enemies they have to hit. They, thinking that they have wealth, might and happiness, think that they are the god.

Addhyo bhijanavan asmi ko nyo sti sadrishomaya
yaksheye dasyami modishya ity agynana vimhitah (15)

I am rich, I am well-born, who is like me, I shall do the sacrifice, I shall bestow, I shall enjoy the pleasures, they think so, mislead/deluded as they out of their ignorance.

Anekachittavibhranta mohajalasamavritah
prasaktah kamabhogeshu patanti narke shuchau (16)

Those, whose mind is wandering in delusions, entangled in the web of allurements and attached to objects of sensual pleasures, they go down to hell.

Atmasambhavitah stabdha dhanamanamadanvitah
yajante namaya gaiste dambhena vidhipurvakam (17)

Clamouring their superiority, without humility, driven with money and vanity, they carry out sacrifices/rituals for namesake, disregarding laws of tradition.

Ahamkaram balam darpam kamam krodham cha samshritah
mam atama paradeheshu pradvishanto bhyasuyakah (18)

Driven by pride, strength, vanity, lust and anger, when they criticise (assail) others they in fact despise/attack Me (being omnipresent) in the body of the assailed.

Tanaham dvishatah kruran samsareshu naradhaman
kshipamy ajasaram ashubhan asurish eva yonishu (19)

I keep hurling these cruel perpetraters of sin back into the world, sending them to the devilish categories again and again.

Asurim yonim apanna mudha janamani janamani
mamparyapyaiva kaunteya tato yanty adhamam gatim (20)

O Kauntey ! Remaining dull minded and ignorant, they never attain Me, instead, they slide down to the lowest state of hell.

Trividham naraksyedam dvaram nashanam atmanah
kamah krodhas tatha lobhas tasmad etat tryam tyajet (21)

Lust, anger and greed are the three gates to hell brings about the ruination of the soul. Therefor om should avoid these three.

Etair vimuktah kaunteya tamodvarais tribhir narah
acharaty atmanah shreyas tato yati param gatim (22)

O Arjuna ! One who is away from these gates of hell, and conducts himself in a noble manner reaches the supreme stage.

Yah shastravidhim utsrjya vartate kamakaratah
na sa siddhim avapnoti na sukham na param gatim (23)

One who abandons the traditional laws of conduct and acts as he feels like, attains neither perfection, or the supreme, nor even peace.

Tasmach chastram pramanam tekarya akarya vyavasthitau
gyatva shastra vidhan uktam karma kartu miharha asi (24)

Action and inaction are proved/indicated by the traditional laws. Let them guide you for you deserve to work as per law established by the tradition.

CHAPTERX VII

Shri Krishna describes how the people with goodness, i.e., satvic, those with passion, i.e., rajasic and those who are given to darkness, i.e., tamasic, conduct themselves in their day to day lives. Their natures are reflected in the reasons, and in the way the three perform the rituals, eat food, give alms, pray and make efforts. The satvic persons accomplish all these actions with faith, without ego or motive, feeling that it has to be done as a duty. They work with internal peace and towards the universal well being.

Arjuna uvacha

Ye shastravidhim utsrajya yajante shraddhayan vitah
tesham nishtha tu ka krishna sattvam aho rajas tamah (1)

Arjuna said-O Krishna ! Those who conduct sacrifice with faith, although without following the established rites/laws, is their sacrifice satvic, rajasic or tamasic ?

Shri Bhagavan uvacha

Trividha bhavati shraddha dehinam sa svabhavaja
sattviki rajasi chaiva tamsi cheti tam shrinu (2)

Shri Krishna said-Faith of men is of three types viz. satvic, rajasic and tamasic. This is also born out of nature, i.e., it is natural.

Sattvanurupa sarvasya shraddha bhavati bharata
shradhamayo yam purusho yo yachchraddhah sa eva sah (3)

O Bharata ! As is the nature of the soul so would be the person, and so would be the nature of his faith.

Yajante sattvika devan yaksharakshamsi rajasah
pretan bhutaganamsh chanye yajante tamasa janah (4)

Satvic people worship god, rajasic people worship the idols of passion and tamasic people worship the forces of darkness.

Ashastravihitam ghoram tapyante ye tapo janah
dambhahamkarasamyuktah kamaragabalanvitah (5)

Those who conduct sacrifices (exercises of self mortification) disregarding laws, out of hypocrisy and ostentation, with attachment, and complexes of might, they are ignorant people.

Karshayantah sharirastham bhutagramamachetsah
mam chaivantah sharirastham tan viddyasuranishchayan (6)

They only torment the senses and thus they torment Me the dweller. Consider them as of demoniac faith as their intent of violent austerities, not sanctioned by scriptures is only an oppression on the elements of the body and thus to Me.

Aharas tv api sarvasya trividho bhavati priyah
yagyas tapas tatha danam tesham bhedarmimam shrnu (7)

Born out of nature, the food habits are also of three types. So are the sacrifices, penance (practice of ascetic devotion), and gift of alms. I will tell you distinctly about these.

Ayuh sattvabalarogya sukhapritivivardhanah
rasyah snigdhah sthira hradya aharah satvikapriyah (8)

Satvic people like foods which promote good health, age, strength, happiness, pleasant feelings and are naturally agreeable.

Katvamlalavanatyushana tikshnarukshvidahinah
ahara rajasayasyeshta dukha shokamayapradah (9)

Rajasic people like foods which are bitter, pungent, salty, spicy, dry and hot. They cause pain, diseases and sadness.

Yatayamam gatarasam putiparyushitam cha yat
uchchishtam api cha medhyam
bhojanam tamasapriyam (10)

Food that is stale, without flavour, foul smelling, cold and impure, such food is dear to the *Tamasic* people.

Aphalakangkshibhir yagyo vidhidrshto ya ejyate
yashtavyam eveti manah samadhaya sa sattvikah (11)

Sacrifice done with the steadfastness of a duty and without desires, according to the rites is a Satvic sacrifice.

Abhisamdhaya tu phalam dambhartham api chaiv yat
ejyate bharatshreshtha tam yagyam viddhi rajasam (12)

O Arjuna ! Sacrifice done with the desire to obtain fruits and for vain display, such a sacrifice is Rajasic.

Viddhihinam asrishtannam mantrahinam adakshinam
shraddhavirahitam yagyam tamasamparichkshate (13)

Tamasic sacrifice is one that is done without rites, without solemnity and without faith or charity.

Devadvijaguru pragya pujanam shaucham arjavam
brahmacharyamahinsa cha shariram tapa uchyate (14)

True penance of body is reverence to gods, teacher, brahmin and the wise. It is a practice of purity, simplicity, chastity and non-violence.

Anudvegakaram vakyam satyam priyahitam cha yat
svaaddhyayabhyasanam chaiva
vangamayam tapa uchayate (15)

Penance of the tongue is truthful speech, which does not hurt, is pleasing, helpful and given to sacred recitations.

Manah prasadah saumyatvam maunam atmavinigrahah
bhavasamshuddhirity etat tapo manasam uchayate (16)

Penance of mind is serenity, amiability, reticence, self-control, internal purity and sense of well being/ bliss/contentment.

Shraddhaya paraya taptam tapas tat trividhim naraih
aphalakangkshibhir yuktaih satvikam parichakshayate (17)

So are done, the three types of penance, by the satvic people, with faith and without desires.

Satakaramanapujartham tapo dambhena chaiv yat
kriyate tadiha proktam rajasam calam adhruvam (18)

Penance of rajasic is to gain reverence, eminence, and for popularity (show). It is fickle and does not stay.

Mudhagrahenatamano yatapidya kriyate tapah
parasyotsadanartham va tat tamasam udahritam (19)

Penance of tamasic is out of perversion, foolishness and obstinacy. It is with torture to mind, voice and body or for ruin to others.

Datavyam iti yad danam diyate nupakarine
deshe kale cha patre cha taddanam sattvikam smartam (20)

Satvic gift is giving of alms as a sense of sacred duty, to a deserving recipient, from whom no return is possible (no return can be expected) at the right time and at the right place.

Yat tu pratyukarartham phalam uddishya va punah
diyate cha pariklishtam tad danam
rajahansam smritam (21)

Rajasic gift is given with pain/hesitation, with expectation of return, for the sake of/intention towards the fruits of the action (of piety/benediction).

Adeshakale yaddanam apatrebhyash cha diyate
asatkritam avagyatam tat tamasamudahritam (22)

Tamasic gift is made to an unworthy recipient, at the wrong place and time, with disrespect and contempt.

Ohm tat saditi nirdesho brahmanas tri vidhah smritah
brahmanastena vedashcha yagyashcha vihitah pura (23)

Ohm, tat, sat, are the three names (symbols) of Brahma. The scriptures like the Vedas were written by it at the time of creation. **

Ohm is for absolute supremacy of Brahma, tat is for universality which is beyond existence, and sat is the reality of Brahma, which is existent.

Tasmad om ity udahrtya yagya dana tapah kriyah
pravartante vidhanoktah satatam brahmavadinam (24)

And so all the acts of sacrifice, penance and alms giving, conducted by great men, as per tradition begin with the chant of *ohm,* the name of god.

Tad ity anabhisamdhaya phalam yagyatapah kriyah
danakriyash cha vividhah kriyante
mokshakangkshibhih (25)

Those who want salvation, so pronounce *tat,* the name of god, in all their acts of sacrifice, penance and alms giving, without being concerned for the fruits of their acts.

Sadbhave sadhubhave cha sad ity etat prayujyate
prashaste karmani tatha sach chabdah partha yujyate (26)

Sat, the name of god, is to be used for all that is sacred, praiseworthy and sublime. O Parthe ! In doing good work also, the word sat is used.

Yagye tapasi dane cha sthitih sad iti chochyate
karma chaiv tadarthiyam sadity eva bhidhiyate (27)

Sat means being eager and assiduous in sacrifice, penance and charity. Works done for the supreme being is also *sat,* so it is said.

Ashraddhya hutam dattam tapstaptam kritam cha yat
asad ity uchyate partha na cha tatpryetya no iha (28)

O Arjuna ! Sacrifice, charity or devotion, whatever good work is done without faith is not *sat* (it is asat) and such works are no good either in this world or the next.

CHAPTER XVIII

It is the motive behind the action, not the action itself which decides the nature of the action. Actions loaded with expectations are not desirable. Similarly, renunciation done out of fear, or as a solution to a problem is mere abdication. It is impossible for any living being to totally abstain from action. The wise person performs actions as a duty, as a thing which ought to be done, renouncing all attachment to the act well as to its consequences/fruits. He has neither attachment to good actions nor aversion to disagreeable ones which he may be compelled to do.

The factors of an action are the self, the mind, the body, its faculties and the destiny. Those who do not perceive these feel that they (the individual) are the only factor. However those who understand this, that all are bound by their own nature and their destiny, become free of the ego of being the doer and thus can never do any wrong. The person with unaffected mind, living a pure life, acting without attachment or ego establishes unison with existence, a harmony with the universe and thus attains peace.

The discourse of Shree Bhagavad Gita concludes with Arjuna confessing that all his doubts stand clear and he is ready to fulfill his duty of the hour by entering the battlefield of Kurukshetra.

Arjuna uvacha

Sannyasasya mahabaho tattvam ichchami veditum
tyagasya cha hrishikesha prithak keshinishudana (1)

Arjuna said— strong armed (Shri Krishna) ! O omniscient ! O Vasudeva ! I want to understand the essence of renunciation (sanyas) and relinquishment/ sacrifice separately.

Shri bhagavana uvacha

Kamyanam karmanam nyasam sanyasam kavayo vidhuh
sarva karma phala tyagam prahustyagam vichakshanah (2)

Shri Bhagawan (Krishna) said- Some wise men feel that renunciation is abstention from works, actions prompted by desire, even which need to be done, and some wise men feel that relinquishment/ sacrifice is the abandonment of the results of the action.

Tyajyam doshavad ityeke karma prahurmanishinah
yagyadanatapah karma na tyajyam iti chapre (3)

Some learned men say that action itself is contaminated and so deserves to be abstained from, while the others feel that (pious) actions concerning sacrifice, charity and penance need not be given up.

Nishchayam shrinu me tatra tyage bharatasattama
tyago hi purushavyaghra trividhah samprakirtitah (4)

O foremost among men Arjuna ! Between renunciation and relinquishment, I shall tell you the truth about relinquishment (sacrifice) first because it is said to be of three types viz. *satvic, rajasic* and *tamasic.*

Yagya dana tapah karma na tyajyam karyam eva tat
yagyo danam tapash chaiv pavanani manishinam (5)

Actions such as sacrifice, gift and penance are essential, rather a duty, as they purify the intelligent person, and hence should not be given up.

Yetany api tu karmani sangam tyaktva phalani cha
kartavyaniti me partha nishchitam matam uttamam (6)

As such O Parthe ! I do believe that all such dutiful actions, and the ones which have got to be done, should be done but without attachment and abjuring the fruits of the actions.

Niyatasya tu sanyasah karmano no papadyate
mohattasya parityagas tamasah pari kirtitah (7)

Abstention from assigned works is not desirable, and so relinquishment of a regular duty, done out of ignorance, is a *tamasic* sacrifice.

Duhkham ity eva yat karma kayakleshabhayat tyajet
sa kritva rajasam tyagam naiva tyagaphalam labhet (8)

Work is a form of trouble, thinking so, if someone gives up his dutiful works out of fear of physical pains, such a sacrifice is rajasic sacrifice and there is nothing to gain from such a sacrifice.

Karyam ity eva yat karma niyatam kriyate arjuna
sangam tyaktva phalam chaiv sa tyagah satviko matah (9)

But O Arjuna ! Dutiful action done, considering them as one's own duty, without attachment and without desire of the fruits of the action, is itself a satvic sacrifice.

Na dveshtya akushalam karma kushale nanushjjate
tyagi satvasamavishto medhavi chinnasamshayah (10)

The person who has no repugnance to distasteful works (which are needed to be done for the continuance of the world system) and similarly has no attraction towards agreeable actions, he is the pure, firm, intelligent and a true sacrificer.

Na hi dehabhriatashakyam tyaktum karmany asheshatah
yas tu karma phalatyagi sa tyagitya abhidhiyate (11)

Since it is impossible for any living being to give up actions altogether, one who gives up the fruits of action is one who has truely relinquished, so it is said.

Anishtamishtam mishram cha trividham karmanah phalam
bhavatyatyaginam pretya na tu sanyasinam kvachit (12)

One who does not give up the fruits of his works gets good, mixed and bad results at last, but one who has given up the fruits of actions never gets them at any time (does not have to bear the results, good or the bad, at all).

Panchaitani mahabaho karaninibodha me
sankhye kritante prokttani siddhaye sarvakarmanam (13)

O strong armed (Arjuna) ! Also understand clearly the five factors which cause the accomplishment of all actions, as described in the Sankhya philosophy.

Adhish tanam tatha karta karanam cha prithagvidham
vividhash cha prithakcheshta daivam chaivatra
panchamam (14)

These five factors are—The scene of action (i.e. body/material basis), the doer, the instruments of various sorts, (i.e., the sensory organs and mind, the faculties with which the action is performed), the many kinds of efforts, (i.e., the motions which create activities/impulses in the mind and the senses), and providence, (i.e., divine factors).

Shariravangamnobhir yat karma prarabhate narah
nyayayam va vipritam va panchaite tasya hetavah (15)

These are the five factors which cause all the actions man does with mind, speech and body, whether good, bad, or otherwise.

Tattraivam sati karamtarm atmanam kevalam tu yah
pashyatya akritbuddhitvam na sa pashyati durmati (16)

In spite of this fact, still if a person, out of contorted intellect, feels that only the pure self is the doer of the actions (considers himself as the one who is doing), he is ignorant and does not understand the truth.

Yasya nahamkrito bhavo buddhir yasya na lipyate
hatvapi sa imaml lokanan na hanti na nibaddhyate (17)

He who does not feel in himself that he is the doer (being without ego), and whose mind is not involved/attached to earthly things or to works, such a person neither slays (even if he has killed the whole world) nor is he bound by/to any sin/action.

Gyanam gyeyam parigyata trividha karmachodana
karnam karma karteti trividhah karmasangrahah (18)

Knower, knowledge and knowing are the three inspirations to action. The doer, the implement/instrument and the act, these are the three constituents of action.

Gyanam karma chakarta ca tridhaiva gunabhedatah
prochyate gunasankhyane yathavachchranu tany api (19)

The qualities of the knowledge, the doer and the work have been analysed as being of three types. You must also know about them well.

Sarvabhuteshu yenaikam bhavam avyayam ikshate
avibhaktam vibhakteshu tajygyanam viddhi satvikam (20)

The satvic knowledge is knowledge of purity and goodness i.e by which man sees the one Supreme imperishable, established indivisibly and with an equal mind/effect (without preferences) among divergent existences/beings.

Prithaktvena tu yaj gyanam nanabhavan aprithagvidhan
vetti sarveshu bhuteshu tajyagyanam viddhi rajasam (21)

The knowledge which distinguishes between beings, i.e., by which one understands the various characters/qualities in the various beings, in separation and distinction, is the wisdom of passion i.e. rajasic knowledge.

Yat tu kritsnavad ekasminkarye saktam ahaitukam
atattvartha vadalpam cha tat tamasamudahirtam (22)

And the knowledge, which is confined to the attachment of one's body, as if it is everything, which is irrational, of no utility and meaningless, such knowledge is out of darkness, i.e., it is *tamasic* knowledge.

Niyatam sangarahitam aragadveshatah kritam
aphalaprepsuna karma yat tat sattvikam uchyate (23)

The work which is sanctified as duty by law, which is without the expectations of the fruit of the action, which is done without attachment, envy or pride of being the doer, such action is pure, i.e., satvic.

Yat tu kamepsuna karma sahamkarena va punah
kriyate bahulayasam tad rajasam udahritam (24)

Work which is done with great effort, by men with ego, and done for the pleasures of the fruits of the effort, such work is of passion, i.e., it is rajasic.

Anubandham kshayam hinsamanavekshya cha paurusham
mohadarabhyate karma yat tat tam asamuchyate (25)

Work initiated without the thought of the consequences, losses, dangers and capabilities, with sheer ignorance, is the work of darkness, i.e., it is *tamasic* action.

Muktasango nahamvadi dhrityutsahasamanvitah
siddhyasiddhyor nirvikarah karta satvika uchyate (26)

The worker who is without attachments and without complexes of ego, who is patient, zealous, and unaffected by the joys and sorrows of success and failure, such a worker is called a *satvic* worker.

Ragi karmaphalaprepsurlabdho hinsatmako shuchi
harshashokanvitah karta rajasah parikirtitah (27)

The worker who has attachments, who desires the fruits of actions, who is greedy, inclined to hurt others, depraved, and moved by joy and woe, he is a worker of passion, i.e., *rajasic*.

Ayuktah prakritah stabdhah shato naishkritiko lasah
vishadi dhirghasutri cha karta tamasa uchyate (28)

He who is inept, uneducated, proud, cheat, apathetic to other beings, mournful, lazy and procrastinator, he the worker of darkness, i.e., he is a *tamasic* worker.

Buddherbhedam dhrvatesh chaiva
gunatastrividham shranu
proychyamanam asheshena pristhaktvena dhananjaya (29)

O Dhananjaya ! Intellect and patience are also divided into threefold categorisation according to their qualities. Hear about the nuances of each of them.

Pravritim cha nivrittim cha karyakarye bhayabhaye
bandham moksham cha ya vetti buddhih sa partha
sattviki (30)

O Partha ! The intellect which knows about works/actions that have to be done and those that need not be done, about dutiful action and inaction, about fear and fearlessness, about bondage and liberation, such intellect is the intellect of the pure, i.e., *satvic*.

Yaya dharmamadharmam cha karyam cha karyam eva cha
ayathavatprajanati buddhih sa partha rajasi (31)

O Partha ! The intellect which does not truly know what is righteous and what is wrong, what is dutiful and what ought not to be done, such intellect is *rajasic*.

Adharmam dharmam iti ya manyate tamasavrita
sarvarthana viparitamsh cha buddhih sa partha tamasi (32)

O Arjuna ! The mind, stooped in ignorance, which considers wrong as righteous, and thinks everything in the opposite (negative/perverted) way, is the *tamasic* mind.

Dhritya yaya dharayate manah pranendriya kriyah
yogenaavyabhicharinya dhritih sa partha sattviki (33)

O Partha ! The perseverance with which man holds fast to the works of mind, body and senses, by the practice of concentration, for the conduct of detached actions, is *satvic* steadfastness.

Yaya tu dharma kamarthaan dhritya dharayate arjuna
prasangena phalakangkshi dhritih sa partha rajasi (34)

O Arjuna ! the relove by which a man, craving for the fruits of work, clings to duty, wealth and success, earthly possessions worldly enjoyments with great attachment that resolve, is Rajasika.

Yaya svapanam bhayam shokam vishadam madam eva cha
na vimunchati durimedha dhratih sa partha tamasi (35)

O Partha ! The firmness by which an evil minded person refuses to shake of, i.e, clings to sleep, fear, anxiety, sorrow, and excitement, such power of bearing is tamasic.

Sukham tvidanim trividham shranu me bhararshabh
abhyasadramate yatra dukhantam cha nigachchati (36)

Yat tad agre visham iva parinamemritopamam
tat sukham satvikam proktam atmabuddhi prasadajam (37)

Happiness is also of three types. Cheerfulness with which a person rejoices the practice of devotion, meditation and service, which is enjoyed after much effort, which ends suffering, which may have appeared difficult at the start but turns out to be good in the end, which is out of one's own intellect (self-contentment/fulfilment) is satvic happiness.

Vishyendriya sangyogaad yat tad agre mritopamam
pariname vishamiva tatsukham rajasam smritam (38)

The happiness which arises out of union of objects of pleasure and senses, which is pleasing in the beginning but ends up in sadness, is rajasic happiness.

Yad agre chanubandhe cha sukham mohanam atmanah
nidralasya pramadottham tat tamasam udayahritam (39)

What is delusory from begining to the end, which comes from somnolence, lethargy and intoxication, such happiness is tamasic happiness.

Na tad asti prithivyam va divi deveshu va punah
sattvam prakritijairmuktam yad
ebhih syatribhir gunaih (40)

There is no being, either on the earth or in the heaven, moving or fixed, anywhere, who is without these three qualities/constituents created by nature.

Brahmanakshatriyavisham shudranam cha paramtapa
karmani pravibhaktani svabhava prabhavair gunaih (41)

O Arjuna ! The works/assignments of the brahmins, the kshatriyas, the vaishyas and the shudras have been divided in accordance with the qualities created out of their nature.

Shamo damas tapah shaucham kshantir arjavam eva cha
gyanam vigyanam astikyam
brahmakarma svabhavajam (42)

Inner calm, self-control, purity, integrity, uprightness, penance, forgiveness, simplicity, wisdom, knowledge and faith are the works/duties intrinsic to brahmins.

Shauryam tejo dhritir dakshyam yuddhe chapy apalayanam
danam ishvarabhavash cha
kshatram karma svabhavajam (43)

Valour, ardour, forbearance, tact, perseverance in battle (adversity), charity and leadership are natural works/activities to kshatriyas.

Krishigaurakshyavanijyam vaishya karma svabhavajam
paricharyatmakam karma shudrasyapi svabhavajam (44)

Farming, cow rearing and fair trade are natural duties of vaishyas. Service to others is natural work of shudras.

Sve sve karmanya abhiratah samsiddhim labhate narah
svakarmaniratah siddhim yatha vindati tach chranu (45)

One who is constantly/eagerly engaged in the works of his natural duty attains divine-like state of supreme perfection. How he attains the state of supreme perfection by performing his natural duties, listen about that system.

Yatah pravrittir bhutanam yen sarvam idam tatam
svakarmana tam abhyarcya siddhim vindati manavah (46)

He, who is the creator of all, who pervades the entire existence, His dedicated worship through the performance of one's own natural works, leads one to supreme perfection.

Shreyan svadharmo vigunah paradharmat svanushthitat
svabhavaniyatam karma kurvan na pnoti kilbhisham (47)

Better is one's own law / duty, even though of less value, than (adopting/following) another person's law/duty, even if well conducted, because by adhering to the dutiful works decided by one's own nature, one incurs no sin. One does no wrong if one is sincere to one self than being hypocritical.

Sahajam karma kaunteya sadosham api na tyajet
sarvarambha hi doshena dhumenagnirivavritah (48)

As such O son of Kunti ! Even if the works, natural (suited) to one, have any deficiency, they should still not be given up, because there is no work/action which is free of deficiencies.

Asaktabuddhih sarvatra jitatma vigatasprihah
naishkarmya siddhim paramam
sannyasenadhigachchati (49)

With intellect free of complexes, control over body, senses and mind, one whose works are without desires achieves the supreme perfection of being the non-doer, the state which transcends all work.

Siddhim prapto yatha brahma tatha pnoti nibodha me
samasenaiva kaunteya nishtha gyanasya ya para (50)

Having achieved such perfection, how one attains brahma, which is the finale/pinnacle of wisdom, listen about it briefly, O son of Kunti.

Buddhya vishuddhaya yukto dhrityatmanam niyamya cha
shabdadinvishyamstyaktva ragadveshau vyudasya ca (51)

Viviktasevi laghvashi yatavakkayamanasah
dhyanayogaparo nityam vairagyam samupashritah (52)

One with pure mind, patience and self-control, abjuring pleasures of senses, without fondness, hatred or passion, let him be in solitude, freshness and serenity, let him be frugal and regular in meals, controlling mind, tongue and body with satvic perseverance, let him be always integrated with self, let him practice meditation and renunciation.

Ahamkaram balam darpam kamam kradham parigraham
vimuchya nirmamah shanto brahmabhuyaya kalpate (53)

Forsaking complexes of pride, conceit, power, lust, anger and possession, with steadfastness and tranquility, free of the thought of anything being 'mine', he conforms to attain the status of Brahma.

Brahmabhutah prasannatma na shochati na kangkshati
samah sarveshu bhuteshu madbhaktim labhate param (54)

With concentration devoted completely towards *brahma,* the pleasant feeling *yogi* neither grieves for anyone, nor expects from anyone. Such a *yogi* who has the sameness of feeling towards everyone achieves to the supreme devotion to me.

Bhaktya mam abhijanati yavan yash chasmi tattvatah
tato mam tattvato gyatva vishate tadanantaram (55)

By that supreme devotion, he understands the Supreme Me in essence, who I am and how much I am, and by that devotion he gets integrated into with my form.

Sarvakarmamya api sada kurvano madvyapashrayah
matprasadad avapnoti shashvatam padam avyayam (56)

My devoted karma-yogi (one who depends/ trusts on me), even while performing all the works regularly, attains my eternal and imperishable supreme state.

Chetsa sarvakarmani mayi samnyasya matpara
buddhiyogamupashritya machchitah satatam bhava (57)

As such Arjuna , mentally relieve yourself by dedicating/offering all works/actions into Me, and following the doctrine of equal mindedness, abide by Me, and keep your mind always fixed towards Me.

Machchitah sarvadurgam matprasadat tarishyasi
atha chet tvamahamkaran nashroshyasi vinangkshyasi (58)

By trusting Me in the way described, by My grace you will surpass all pains and obstacles without any effort. If you will ignore My words out of vanity you shall meet with destruction (you would be distracted from the noble path).

Yadahamkaramashritya na yotsya iti manyase
mithyaish vyavasayaste prakritis tvam niyokshyati (59)

Out of vanity that you think 'I will not fight' but your resolution is illusory. Your nature will forcibly assign you to battle.

Svabhavajena kaunteya nibaddhah svena karmana
kartum nechchasi yanmohat karishyasyavsho api tat (60)

O son of Kunti ! The work which you are not willing to do out of attachment, you will be compelled to do, being bound by your nature. The attachment to your loved ones is also a creation of the work of your nature, due to which you are not willing to fight, but by the forces/works of the same nature you will yourself be compelled to fight, inspite of yourself.

Ishvarah sarvabhutanam hriddeshe arjuna tishthati
bhramayansarvabhutani yantrarudani mayaya (61)

O Arjuna ! Riding the body like an instrument, the omnipresent Supreme One, dwelling inside everyone, moves all the beings by His power of maya according to their works.

Tam eva sharanam gachcha sarvabhavena bharata
tatprasadatparam shantim sthanam prapsyasi shashvatam (62)

O Arjuna ! Take complete refuge in Him. Only by His grace you shall achieve lasting peace and eternally supreme abode.

Iti te gyanamakhyatam guhyad guhayataram maya
vimrashyai tad asheshena yathechchasi tatha kuru (63)

So I have told you the most esoteric of esoteric knowledge. Now think over this mysterious wisdom thoroughly, and then do exactly as you want.

Sarvaguhvatamam bhuyah shrinu me paramam vachah
ishtoasi me dridhamiti tato vakshyami te hitam (64)

Hear yet again the most secret of My secret words. As you are extremely dear to Me, I shall repeat to you these words of supreme benefit.

Manmana bhava madbhakto madyaji mam namaskuru
mamevaishasi satyam te pratijane priyo asi me (65)

O Arjuna ! Think of Me, be My devotee, worship Me, greet Me. As you are very dear to Me, I truly avow that by doing so you will attain Me only.

Sarvadharmanparityajya mam ekam sharanam vraja
aham tva sarvapapebhyo mokshyishyami ma shuchah (66)

Relinquish (dedicate/relieve yourself of) all yours duties (everything) into Me, and come in My shelter.

I shall liberate/deliver you out of your sins (bonds of karma). Do not grieve.

Idam te natapaskaya nabhaktaya kadachana
na chashushrushave vachyam na cha mam yo
abhyasuyati (67)

You should never tell this mysterious sermon to one who is without penance, who is without faith (devotion), and to one who is not interested in listening. Also to one who sees fault in Me these words should never be said.

Ya imam paramam guhyam madbhakateshav abhidhasyati
bhaktim mayi param kritva mam evaishyaty
asamsayah (68)

One who will relate this secret knowledge to My devotees, out of his devotion to Me, shall achieve Me, there is no doubt about it.

Na cha tasmana manushyeshu kashchin me priyakrittamah
bhavita na cha me tasmadanyah priyataro bhuvi (69)

There neither is, nor shall ever be in future, any person dearer to Me than one who does My service so.

Adhyeshyate cha ya imam dharmyam samvadam avayoh
gyanyagyena tenahamishtah syamiti me matih (70)

He who studies this discourse of ours, Gita which is full of righteousness, by him also I shall be worshipped through the exercise of wisdom, so do I opine.

Shraddhavan anasuyashch shrinuyadapi yo narah
so api muktah shubhaml lokanprapnuyat
punyakarmanam (71)

He who even listens to this discourse of Gita, with faith and without a view to fault finding, also achieves liberation from his sins (troubles) and reaches the world of those who do good works.

Kachchid tachchutam partha tvayaikagrena chetasa
Kachchidgyansammohah pranashtste dhananjaya (72)

O Partha ! Did you hear this discourse with full attention Arjuna ? And O Dhananjaya ! Is your enchantment caused out of ignorance gone ?

Arjuna uvacha

Nashto mohah smritir labdha tvatprasadanmayachyuta
sthitho smi gatasandehah karishye vachanam tava (73)

Arjuna said-O Achyuta ! Due to your grace my misimpression/delusion is destroyed and I have regained memory (the power of discernment). I stand firm and stable, without any doubts, and so I shall do as You tell me.

Sanjaya uvacha

Ity aham vasudevasya parthasya cha mahatmanah
samvadamm imam ashrausham adbhutam
romaharshanam (74)

Sanjaya said-So did I hear the fascinating, deep and exciting discourse between Shri Vasudeva and Mahatma Arjuna.

Vyasa prasadachch etad guhyam aham vanetadguhrmaham
param
yogam yogeshvaratkrishanatsakshat kathayatah
svayam (75)

By the grace of sage Vyas who endowed me with paternatural vision, I myself heard this esoteric wisdom of yoga from Krishna as He said it in person.

Rajan samsmritya samsmritya samvadam imam adbhutam
keshavarjunayoh punyam hrishyami
cha muhur muhah (76)

O King ! Recollecting this mystifying, beneficial and marvellous discourse between Krishna and Arjuna pleases me no end.

Tach cha samsmritya samsmritya
rupam atyadbhutam hareh
vismayo me mahan rajanhrishyami cha punah punah (77)

O King ! As many times as I recall the sight of the divine form of Shri Krishna, I am filled with amazement and joyous thrill.

Yatra yogeshavarh krishno yatra partho dhanurdharah
tatra shrir vijayo bhutirdhruva nitirmatirmama (78)

O King ! I am convinced that wherever is Yogeshwar Shri Krishna and Arjuna, bearer of Gandiva, there is victory, prosperity, eternal fortune and sound policy.

INDEX